UPDATED EDITION

DIGITAL TRANSFORMATION

JULIAN DELPHIKI

DIGITAL TRANSFORMATION IN AN EVER-CHANGING WORLD

Digital transformation guidelines and how to create a digital marketing strategy

- Julian Delphiki -

Copyright © 2025 Julian Delphiki

All rights reserved. No part of this publication may be reproduced, distributed, or transmitted in any form or by any means, including photocopying, recording, or other electronic or mechanical methods, without the prior written permission of the publisher, except in the case of brief quotations embodied in critical reviews and certain other noncommercial uses permitted by copyright law.

Digital Transformation in an ever-changing world / Julian Delphiki – 1st Edition

ISBN 979-8647451002

INDEX

INTRODUCTION

THE ADVENT OF AI, AUTOMATION AND ROBOTIZATION

WHAT IS DIGITAL TRANSFORMATION?

PREPARING FOR CHANGE

DIGITAL TRANSFORMATION SUCCESS STORIES

THE TRANSFORMATION ITSELF

- INTRODUCTION
- DIGITAL VISION AND LEADERSHIP
- WHAT TO TRANSFORM
- DIGITAL TRANSFORMATION AS HUMAN TRANSFORMATION

A PRACTICAL APPROACH TO A DIGITAL TRANSFORMATION

- INTRODUCTION
- BUILDING AN ENGAGEMENT STRATEGY
- TRACKING YOUR PROGRESS
- WHAT DOES SUCCESS LOOK LIKE?

SUMMARY

A HOLISTIC STRATEGY

- INTRODUCTION
- SETTING GOALS AND OBJECTIVES
- THE CUSTOMER JOURNEY
- THE DIGITAL CHANNELS

A BUDGET FOR OUR STRATEGY

BUDGETS AND AGENCY BRIEFS

SUMMARY

GLOSSARY

ABOUT JULIAN DELPHIKI

OTHER BOOKS BY THE AUTHOR

PART I
DIGITAL TRANSFORMATION

INTRODUCTION

Regardless of your job title, role, industry, or sector, It is fairly likely that you will have heard the term 'digital transformation.' In our ever-changing digital world, businesses of all shapes and sizes are met with a challenge to successfully employ new technologies to find a better way of serving their needs. What is becoming clear is that in order to succeed, It is necessary to develop new skills and capabilities, and even new ways of thinking, behaving, and working. In this book, we will be discussing what 'Digital Transformation' is, what it is not, and how you as an individual, team or company can be prepared for change.

THE ADVENT OF AI, AUTOMATION AND ROBOTIZATION

The emergence and convergence of AI, automation, and robotization are set to transform virtually any type of company or job position in profound ways. AI's ability to process vast amounts of data and generate insights will revolutionize decision-making processes across industries. By leveraging machine learning algorithms, businesses can predict market trends, optimize supply chains, and personalize customer experiences with unprecedented accuracy. Automation, on the other hand, will streamline operations, eliminating repetitive tasks and reducing errors. Robotization will extend these efficiencies into the physical realm, particularly in manufacturing and logistics, where robots can perform precise and demanding tasks without fatigue.

This convergence means that even traditionally human-centric roles will see significant changes. In marketing, for instance, AI can analyze consumer behavior data to craft highly targeted campaigns, while automated systems manage ad placements and track performance in real-time. Human marketers will shift from routine tasks to strategic roles, focusing on creative and innovative initiatives. Similarly, in finance, AI-driven analytics can assess risk, detect fraud, and provide financial advice, transforming the roles of financial analysts and advisors. Automation will handle transactions and compliance, freeing professionals to focus on higher-level financial planning and client relations.

Healthcare will experience a revolution through this convergence as well. AI can diagnose diseases from medical images with high accuracy, suggest personalized treatment plans, and predict patient outcomes. Automation in administrative tasks will reduce the burden on healthcare providers, allowing them to spend more time with patients. Robotization will assist in surgeries and patient care, performing tasks that require precision and consistency. These advancements will enhance the quality of care, reduce costs, and improve patient outcomes.

In the realm of manufacturing, the integration of AI, automation, and robotization will create smart factories where machines communicate and collaborate seamlessly. Predictive maintenance powered by AI will minimize downtime and optimize productivity. Automated systems will manage inventory, production schedules, and quality control, ensuring efficiency and consistency. Robots will handle the physical assembly and packaging of products, performing tasks that are dangerous or tedious for humans. This will not only increase output but also improve workplace safety.

Even sectors like education and hospitality will see transformations. AI can personalize learning experiences, providing real-time feedback and tailoring curricula to individual students' needs. Automation will streamline administrative tasks such as enrollment, grading, and scheduling. In hospitality, AI can enhance guest experiences through personalized recommendations and efficient service management, while robots can assist with cleaning, food delivery, and even concierge services.

The impact on job positions will be significant. Routine and repetitive tasks will be increasingly handled by AI and automated systems, while roles requiring creativity, critical thinking, and emotional intelligence will become more valuable. Employees will need to adapt by developing new skills and embracing lifelong learning. Companies will need to invest in upskilling their workforce and redesigning job roles to leverage human strengths in conjunction with AI and automation.

In summary, the convergence of AI, automation, and robotization will transform every industry and job position. Companies will achieve greater efficiency, accuracy, and innovation, while employees will need to adapt to new roles that emphasize human creativity and problem-solving. This transformation promises a future where technology and human ingenuity work hand-in-hand to drive progress and improve lives.

AI is not the same as robotization, except if you're a knowledge worker. For most people, AI doesn't mean robots taking over physical tasks. It's about algorithms processing information, not machines replacing human limbs. Robotization refers to physical robots performing manual tasks, like in manufacturing. AI, however, focuses on data analysis, pattern recognition, and decision-making processes. It's more about software than hardware.

However, if you're a knowledge worker, the lines can blur. Knowledge workers, those who handle information, ideas, and data, are directly impacted by AI. Their tasks often involve analyzing data, interpreting information, or making decisions based on large datasets. AI can enhance or even replace these functions, not by robotic means, but through advanced data processing capabilities. Here, AI acts as an intelligent assistant or sometimes as a superior alternative, analyzing data faster and more accurately than humans.

On the other hand, AI is not synonymous with automation. Automation refers to the use of technology to perform tasks with minimal human intervention. While automation has been around for decades, typically in repetitive and well-defined tasks, AI brings a new level of sophistication. AI-powered automation can handle more complex and variable tasks that traditional automation cannot. However, if your work can be mostly automated, perhaps you're not as much of a knowledge worker as you think. Knowledge work implies a level of cognitive engagement, creativity, and problem-solving that goes beyond routine tasks.

The essence of a knowledge worker's role is to apply their expertise to interpret and create value from information. If AI can automate most of your job, it may indicate that the work is more structured and less creative than typically associated with knowledge work. True knowledge work should involve tasks that require a human touch – critical thinking, nuanced understanding, and innovative problem-solving. If AI can do your job entirely, it suggests the tasks are more routine and less intellectually demanding.

In conclusion, while AI and robotization are distinct concepts, AI does intersect with the work of knowledge workers by automating cognitive tasks. But, being able to automate most of your work could suggest that your job may not be as cognitively demanding or creatively engaging as true knowledge work should be. AI enhances and transforms work, particularly for knowledge workers, but it also redefines what it means to be a knowledge worker in an AI-driven world.

If digitalization meant converting analog processes into digital ones without altering the essence of your business, digital transformation—and now the use of AI, automation, and robotization—goes much further. It fundamentally reshapes the core of your business and can revolutionize entire markets. Digitalization involved adopting new tools to enhance efficiency but left business models largely intact. You scanned documents, digitized records, and streamlined communication. It made your operations faster and more efficient but didn't change what you fundamentally do.

Digital transformation, however, began to dig deeper. It wasn't just about using digital tools but integrating them into every aspect of your business, changing how you operate and deliver value to customers. It meant rethinking products, services, and customer interactions to leverage digital capabilities fully. This transformation required a cultural shift, new strategies, and a willingness to innovate continuously. Businesses had to become more agile, data-driven, and customer-centric. They started to adopt cloud computing, data analytics, and mobile technologies, transforming their value propositions and competitive dynamics.

Now, the integration of AI, automation, and robotization is pushing this transformation even further, altering the very core of businesses. AI brings advanced data processing and decision-making capabilities, enabling companies to predict trends, personalize offerings, and optimize operations with a level of precision previously unattainable. Automation takes over repetitive tasks, reducing costs and errors while freeing human workers for more strategic and creative roles. Robotization extends this automation into the physical domain, particularly in industries like manufacturing and logistics, where robots can perform complex and dangerous tasks with high efficiency and consistency.

These technologies are not just enhancing current business models but are enabling entirely new ones. Consider the retail sector: AI can predict consumer preferences and manage inventory in real-time, while automation and robots handle order fulfillment and delivery. This creates a seamless, highly responsive supply chain that transforms how goods are sold and delivered. Traditional retailers must adapt or risk becoming obsolete, as new market entrants leverage these technologies to offer superior customer experiences.

In finance, AI-driven algorithms can analyze vast datasets to detect fraud, assess creditworthiness, and provide personalized financial advice. Automation can handle transactions and compliance tasks, reducing the need for manual intervention. Financial institutions must rethink their services and business models to stay competitive, offering new digital services and leveraging AI to enhance decision-making and customer engagement.

Healthcare is also being transformed at its core. AI can diagnose diseases with high accuracy, suggest personalized treatment plans, and predict patient outcomes. Automation reduces administrative burdens, while robots assist in surgeries and patient care. These advancements improve patient outcomes, reduce costs, and fundamentally change how healthcare is delivered. Providers must adapt to these changes, integrating new technologies into their practices and rethinking how they interact with patients.

Even traditional industries like agriculture are being transformed. AI and automation can optimize planting and harvesting, monitor crop health in real-time, and manage resources more efficiently. This leads to higher yields and lower costs, changing the very nature of farming. Farmers need to adopt new technologies and practices to stay competitive in this evolving landscape.

While digitalization improved efficiency without altering the core of the business, digital transformation—and now AI, automation, and robotization—go much further. They fundamentally change business models, create new market dynamics, and require a deep rethinking of strategies and operations. Companies that embrace these technologies can unlock new levels of innovation, efficiency, and customer satisfaction, positioning themselves at the forefront of their industries. Those that resist risk being left behind in a rapidly evolving market.

The human impact of using these technologies is unforeseeable. With AI, automation, and robotization, you can do your job in half the time, raising critical questions about the future of work. One immediate concern is whether this increased efficiency will lead to reduced salaries. If your productivity doubles, does it imply your value to the company has halved? Companies might argue that since tasks are completed faster, less time is needed, potentially justifying lower wages. This could lead to a scenario where workers are paid less for what is perceived as less effort, even though the output remains the same.

Alternatively, the focus could shift to increasing production. With these technologies, employees could be expected to double their output, maintaining their current salaries but working at an intensified pace. This approach treats technological advancements as a means to boost productivity rather than reduce labor costs. In such a scenario, workers might face higher performance expectations and increased workloads. The pressure to constantly perform at this enhanced level could lead to stress and burnout, affecting job satisfaction and overall well-being.

Another potential impact is the redefinition of job roles. As routine tasks are automated, employees might be redeployed to more strategic, creative, or complex tasks that cannot be easily automated. This could enhance job satisfaction and provide opportunities for personal and professional growth. However, it requires a significant investment in upskilling and reskilling the workforce. Companies would need to support continuous learning and development to ensure their employees can adapt to new roles and responsibilities. This shift could lead to a more engaged and versatile workforce, but it also raises questions about how these transitions will be managed and who will bear the cost.

Moreover, the social implications of such changes are profound. If businesses increasingly rely on AI and automation, there could be a significant reduction in job opportunities, particularly for lower-skilled positions. This could exacerbate unemployment and widen economic disparities. Society would need to address these challenges through policies that support affected workers, such as social safety nets, retraining programs, and possibly even considering universal basic income to ensure a fair distribution of wealth generated by technological advancements.

Furthermore, the nature of job satisfaction and work-life balance could be transformed. With more time saved through automation, employees might enjoy a better work-life balance, having more time for personal pursuits and family. On the other hand, the blurring of boundaries between work and personal time due to increased connectivity and expectations for constant availability could lead to stress and burnout. Companies and workers will need to navigate these dynamics carefully to ensure that the benefits of increased efficiency do not come at the cost of employee well-being.

The human impact of AI, automation, and robotization -and overall of the digital transformation-, is complex and multifaceted. While these technologies can dramatically increase efficiency, they also raise significant questions about wages, productivity expectations, job roles, and social implications. Whether the outcome will be positive or negative depends on how businesses, employees, and society at large choose to manage these changes.

Balancing the benefits of technological advancements with the need for fair compensation, job satisfaction, and social equity will be crucial in shaping a future that leverages technology for the greater good.

WHAT IS DIGITAL TRANSFORMATION?

It is a familiar buzzword, but knowing what 'digital transformation' is, and why it matters, is more than just a 'nice-to-have' for today's businesses. We are witnessing wave after wave of technological innovation, from developments in mobile and social, and more recently to Artificial Intelligence and the super-connected Internet of Things. Every year, we are introduced to a new technology which promises, or sometimes threatens, to dramatically alter our everyday lives.

Increasingly, businesses are under mounting pressure to find ways to adapt in the face of all this change. The stakes are high - get it wrong, and you could end up disappearing from screens and shelves entirely... But get it right by embracing change and taking risks, and you can open new markets, find new customers, and significantly increase the value of your company.

It used to take Fortune 500 companies an average of 20 years to reach a billion- dollar valuation. Newer companies like Uber and Airbnb are managing it in fewer than five years, and have become synonymous with 'digital innovation.'

We can think of Digital Transformation as a two-stage process. First, digital transforms the way the world works, and second, businesses have to transform to fit into this new reality. Even as customers in a digital world, It is easy to see how technology has transformed our lives – from how we communicate, to how we shop, work and play. These changes have created spectacular new opportunities for innovation, but they have also created incredibly high customer expectations for products and services.

Nowadays, we are so used to one-click ordering and hyper-tailored targeting that when companies do not keep up, they quickly seem out of touch and irrelevant. In many sectors, It is not unheard of for a digital upstart to swoop in and provide a comparable or even superior product or service – and if a legacy business cannot keep up, they are likely to see customers vote with their wallets. These disruptors do not set out to beat you at your own game - they change the rules, so you need to be prepared for change.

That said, true transformation is about much more than having a social media strategy, adopting new technologies or hiring a Chief Data Officer. It is a change management program; changing the way you work, changing your product or even changing your business model, in this ever-changing environment.

And that's pretty tough, because humans are naturally suspicious of change - it brings uncertainty, it involves risk and it requires effort!

You might have already noticed waves of digital initiatives coming into play in your own company. Perhaps you are using big data and artificial intelligence to help make decisions or using robotics in your supply chain. Maybe mobile apps have become a central way you deliver your services. Industries changing is nothing new, but in the digital age, these transformations are being incorporated much faster. Businesses today must evolve at speed, keeping shareholders happy and staff employed. So, what are the five qualities needed to thrive in the digital age?

Successful businesses think differently about their customers. It is not just enough to market your product or service - you need to provide the right touchpoints for customers to discover you, evaluate you and buy your products and services without necessarily seeing an advert.

Due to shifts in the customer journey, many companies have had to rethink traditional marketing models and how they approach personalization. In a connected world, potential and existing customers can use any combination of devices, platforms, and media channels to discover, evaluate and purchase products.

Pizza chain Domino's recognized early that it could use the Internet to transform the way it sold pizzas. The unveiling of Domino's Anyware, a digital ordering platform, put the customer at the heart of the company's eCommerce model, and recognized that people do not order the way they used to. Anyware allows customers to order their pizza through their preferred platform - be that by texting or tweeting a pizza emoji, tapping on a smartwatch, or simply by asking Amazon's Alexa. Nowadays, over 50% of all Domino's orders are placed through mobile devices.

Integrating its services across such a wide range of technologies has meant that users can seamlessly engage with the brand wherever and however they choose. And the benefits for Domino's? Vast quantities of data, allowing it to view each customer as an individual, assess buying patterns and to plan far more personalized campaigns that feel relevant. And, most importantly, to drive more sales than ever!

Businesses also need to think differently about their competition. The question is – what is everyone else doing, and how can you break the mold?

In 2008, Airbnb revolutionized the way we think about finding accommodation around the world. Where global hotel chains size up the competitive landscape against other firms and holiday companies, Airbnb was set up by college students looking to solve a problem. They could not pay their rent, so they created an online platform, allowing homeowners to rent out their homes and spare rooms for some extra cash, and giving travelers a more authentic, local experience. Since its humble beginnings, Airbnb has brokered stays for more than 200 million guests, in over 65,000 cities across more than 191 countries – without owning a single hotel.

Digital transformation also requires that you think differently about data. Today, we are faced with unprecedented quantities of data – from every conversation, every purchase – actually, from every single digital interaction. But being successful is not just about collecting endless sets of data; if you can interpret and learn from the data you collect, it can become a key strategic asset to any business.

Have you ever wondered how Starbucks can open up multiple locations in the same town and yet they are all busy? The coffeehouse giant uses big data to determine the potential success of each new location, taking information on the area itself, traffic, and demographic behavior into account. Carrying out market research by analyzing its data before opening a new Starbucks ensures that the company can make an accurate estimation of what the success rate will be, and choose locations based on the chances for revenue growth.

Digital transformation means embracing innovation on a continual basis, which in itself involves embracing a certain level of risk. Changing a single product or service once might act as a temporary solution, but for longer-term sustained success, you'll need to work on a basis of constant iterations, often referred to as Agile working.

At Google, engineers and developers carry out thousands of tests a year on various products to monitor performance, and they test against a very small subset of their audience to keep risks low. And if something doesn't quite work? The key is to learn from it and put those learnings into action next time around.

This kind of flexible workflow allows for cross-functional and cross-discipline teams to work together to produce the best results in the most efficient way possible. In its very nature, agile working is about finding alternative methods if something is not working, rather than getting stuck in a rut. And who knows? By focusing beyond your current business model, and thinking about what customers will want in the next 10 years, rather than just the next 10 months, making changes could be the best thing you can do for your business.

Digital transformation is, above all, about creating value. Successful businesses are learning to focus beyond current business models and have a laser focus on what customers will value further down the line. Future-proofing your business is not just about dealing with what is happening now but about being prepared for the unknown. Digital transformation is about dramatic change. It changes everything about how products are designed, manufactured, sold, delivered, and serviced and businesses need to be prepared to adapt.

It might be tempting, then, to take a 'better than nothing' approach to digital transformation, upgrading a few core areas of your business in the hope of not being left behind. However, as management consulting firm Mckinsey warns, "It is increasingly clear that we are entering a highly disruptive extinction event [...] Many enterprises that fail to transform themselves will disappear [...] Many new and unanticipated enterprises will emerge, and existing ones will be transformed with new business models. The existential threat is exceeded only by the opportunity."

PREPARING FOR CHANGE

So, there are endless opportunities for businesses that are willing and able to transform themselves, but that is not to say that knowing how to successfully implement these changes is straightforward, by any means.

Although technological developments are, arguably, what has propelled digital transformation to the stage it is now – none of the examples we have talked about would have happened without a clear strategy. Digital transformation is about re- imagining and re-inventing your business for tomorrow, and looking to the future.

Like any planning process, you need a vision, a strategy, and a practical action plan. Preparing a strategy will probably make you challenge some of the core assumptions you might have about your existing business model, questioning what customers value in you now, and how that might change in the future. There are four key steps that you need to consider...

Step one is to Agree your Digital Vision. By carrying out a situational analysis of where your business currently stands on areas like customer experience... communication... products and services...and working practices, you can get a holistic view of your current status. There will, of course, be variations of digital maturity across industries, and even across different departments of the same company.

You need to work out where you are relative to your immediate competitors within the same industry. It is a tricky balance, but It is important to understand the drivers of digital transformation in your own category so that you can focus your time, energy, and money on the right areas! You will want to draw from as many sources and viewpoints as possible, from the boardroom all the way to the coalface, in order to minimize the chance that something important has been overlooked. It is also good to review the outcomes (positive and negative) of any previous digital transformation efforts.

Step two is about Defining your Digital Strategy. Once you have understood where you are currently, this stage is about working out how far from your vision you are, and what the role of digital in your company needs to be. When you know this, you can prioritize some initiatives and best use the capabilities, systems, people, and resources in place. Think of this stage as creating a map to guide your transformation. This is as much a case of defining areas that are a lower priority for intervention in order to ensure that key areas are prioritized and important resources do not end up diverted to serve other agendas within your organization. Of course, no plan unfolds exactly as originally envisaged, so It is also crucial to ensure you have a defined process for modifying the project, this can help ensure that the process will not be derailed by ad-hoc changes made without being properly communicated to the rest of the team.

Step three is to Mobilize! This is where it all comes together and you can start to pilot those digital transformation initiatives and embed new processes. Before you get started with this, you will need to make sure everyone is engaged. Every person, across the business, needs to understand the transformation, its importance to the business, believe in it, and know what their role is. It is critical that your plan is properly communicated to everybody responsible for carrying it out. Remember, it does not matter how perfect your plan is if it never fully exists outside of a document on the server… Change is often hard to cope with, so leaders need to step up and keep everyone focused, reminding them of the vision along the way.

Step four is Learn and Adapt. This is where you track and assess how well you are doing, across a range of pre-defined KPIs and parameters. Digital provides us with so many opportunities for accurate measurement and analysis; not taking advantage of these could prove a set-back. And if something is not working as well as you had hoped or if a new technology or competitor comes along, now is the time to change! This should not represent a single cycle of introspection, but rather a culture of continuous improvement.

Whatever business you work in, transformation is upon us. Your job is to work with your teams to build an organization that can respond to this world in constant flux.

Digital transformation is not a one-time project; the digital world is constantly evolving, but It is very much here to stay. Organizations, therefore, need to find ways of approaching this changeable environment, whilst viewing transformation as a long- term investment.

DIGITAL TRANSFORMATION SUCCESS STORIES

Businesses that embrace the opportunities in digital and accelerate their transformation generate better gross margins, better earnings, and better net income than those who have failed to keep pace. This is backed up in studies by Harvard Business School.

However, the reality is that most companies are still figuring this out. It is definitely not too late, but for many, the clock is ticking.

New businesses emerging have been so successful because instead of expanding their scope incrementally from market to market – they are identifying customers' unmet needs, setting up quickly and rigorously using data to predict and create products that their customers want, even if that means going against what they originally set out to do. After all, Amazon started out as an online bookseller, and has since become a leading cloud storage vendor, now even moving into the world of groceries retailing.

For every business that does successfully adapt and embrace digital transformation, it leaves in its wake a trail of businesses that failed and either did not see the opportunities, or did not fully anticipate the changes to come. Blockbuster is a famous example; rigid beliefs from the top down meant the now-bankrupt media entertainment business went from being a business leader to digitally disrupted out of existence within a decade. So, what went wrong?

From the 1980s, Blockbuster dominated the video rental industry. With thousands of retail locations, millions of customers, massive marketing budgets and efficient operations, it made an enormous amount of money from charging late fees to customers who forgot to return their movies on time. When planning their marketing strategies, two main options arose – 'Make the product more convenient for customers,' or 'Get more customers visiting our stores.' At a time when driving customers to physical retail stores remained a tried and tested way of increasing revenue, It is perhaps unsurprising that Blockbuster opted for the latter.

In 1997, Netflix entered the scene, pioneering a very different model. By removing the hassle of retail locations, it lowered costs and could afford to offer its customers greater variety, and on a global scale. Instead of charging customers to rent videos, it offered an online DVD rental service whereby customers could watch a video for as long as they wanted or return it in the post and get a new one delivered through their letterbox. And with no more irritating late fees!

Eventually Blockbuster tried to introduce mail-order movie rentals, and even dabbled with movie streaming, but it was too little, too late. What had made Blockbuster a success in the past was now a liability. Its physical stores and staffing levels were reliant on store-based revenues and the retail giant's leaders were not brave enough to change.

By this time, Netflix's founder, who years before had tried to sell the company rights to – you guessed it, Blockbuster! – had built up the business to global heights in the entertainment world, which has adapted its business model to offer a video streaming service, producing award-winning original films and TV series with millions of subscribers. Even without the recognizable branding and marketing capabilities held by Blockbuster, the combination of low-cost distribution methods, a clear digital vision and not being tied to an outdated legacy model meant that Netflix could spot a gap in the market and swoop in.

Keeping up with Netflix would have meant some tough decisions: reducing costs by closing stores and making staff redundant in favor of lower cost distribution methods. Blockbuster was stuck in the past and increasingly ignorant of the way the world was changing around it. The business became a dinosaur, with size and lack of speed stopping it from being able to compete.

But do not despair. For every example of companies that have fallen by the wayside, there are a number of established businesses that have shown that they can adapt.

One example is Philips. More than 100 years old, the Dutch-based business looked into the future and saw that lightbulbs were unlikely to play a leading role in driving profits in a world of longer-lasting energy-efficient options.

Instead, they recognized an increasing demand for connected home devices. Seeing an opportunity, the business looked to transform itself by developing alternative lighting systems.

The company took less than a year to develop a wireless connected lighting system in its innovation lab. The Philips Hue smart lighting system lets users control their lighting through an app on their phone, via voice assistants like Siri or Alexa, or even by synchronizing it up to other smart home devices such as connected remote controls. All of this constitutes a radical transformation from the old-style incandescent light bulbs the business had once relied on for revenue.

As the business moved away from traditional products and invested in new technologies, it discovered an untapped opportunity in health technology. With an ageing population and the increasing digitization of healthcare, the company saw an opportunity to shift their focus and branch out into a new market. In fact, over the last five years, Philips has transformed itself to become a health focused company, with its lighting products now housed under a standalone company within the Philips brand, Signify.

And Philips has not just transformed its offering of products and services; the internal structure of the business has been transformed too. A 'digital command center' has been created so that expertise and best practice can be shared across the business.

Philips' digital transformation has genuinely changed the shape of how the company does business. By embracing change, being brave and taking calculated risks Philips has succeeded in pivoting its business towards a new revenue opportunity.

A successful digital transformation strategy involves a delicate balance. For every opportunity and possibility, there are also threats and pitfalls to bear in mind. But with the pace of change getting ever-quicker, this is not the time to sit back and wait. It is not an easy journey for any of today's businesses – even the ones that seemed to be in the right place at the right time - but with the right mindset, it poses an exciting challenge for businesses world-wide.

THE TRANSFORMATION ITSELF

INTRODUCTION

As technologies and customer behaviors continue to evolve, the need for digital transformation across industries is becoming more important than ever. In order to really succeed in your transformation efforts, It is not enough to just invest in new equipment and technology; you need to take the time to understand the changes you need to make, and how to get everyone else on board. Digital transformation is, after all, a human endeavor. In this chapter, we are going to focus on identifying what you could transform, and some of the internal changes that could make all the difference.

DIGITAL VISION AND LEADERSHIP

Preparing your business for the digital world does not happen overnight; It is too big a change and it affects everyone. You need a long-term vision to explain the transformation to others, and that starts by understanding where you are and where you need to be.

You might have heard the phrase 'situational analysis' before - in this case, It is the process of asking yourself some critical questions about your current status, in the context of both market and economic trends, and about your competition.

The key is to be honest in your answers - even if It is tough to hear. This should help you identify: what you need to transform, who your most valuable customers will be in the future - and they might well be different to the ones you have right now - and what kind of company you need to become to meet their needs.

Using insights from inside and outside the business, you will need to remain objective and fact-based as you carry out your analysis. This stage can be a little overwhelming, as you are likely to discover a multitude of areas that will need attention.

But remember - the aim of this phase is not to get lost; It is to make these problems digestible by viewing them as individual, manageable opportunities. There are a number of frameworks for carrying out a situational analysis, depending on business' needs, but here are just a few questions you can ask to get started:

Thinking about your business as a whole, what are your strengths and weaknesses? You will want to take advantage of the areas that are already successful, and address those that could be holding you back.

Having a holistic view of your business also means understanding where it fits into the industry as a whole. What is happening in your market and adjacent markets, and what might the industry itself look like in the future?

There is no denying the impact of technology in digital transformation, so you will also want to understand which significant technological advancements could provide an opportunity, and which could prove a threat if your competitors get there first.

And there will always be some logistical issues, so ask yourself what might get in the way of you transforming, whether that's money, talent, shareholders, or anything else!

Using insights from your situational analysis, you can go on to shape your digital transformation vision, clearly laying out your intentions. A digital vision establishes the direction for everyone else to follow, and lays out the responsibility and deliverables.

A great vision is shared and understood by every employee as they carry out their day-to- day work, but crucially, is manifested in the actions, values and goals of the leaders. Change has to start from the top, but something this important needs to be done in consultation with all key parts of the business, from marketing to HR, from IT to product development.

A great vision can usually be written in half a page, or communicated in 60 seconds. It needs to be intellectually solid, but with emotional appeal, and it must be easily understood by the broad range of people that are going to be affected by the change - whether that is a new graduate or your CEO. The vision should be bold and inspiring, but still realistic. Importantly, it should stay true to the heart of the company, and be future- facing enough to allow you to compete successfully going forward.

Apple's clear and inspiring vision was a key factor in it becoming one of the most valuable companies on the planet. Their vision was to change the digital world, "reinventing the mobile phone" and "defining the future of mobile media," "[to bring] the best computing experience ... to consumers around the world." Having established this vision, they created a set of values which shaped how they hired, conducted meetings, rewarded employees and crucially, how they made all business decisions.

Digital transformation visions should go beyond the numbers typically found in five-year plans. And while digital transformation can mean technology, It is also much more than that. It is about transforming ways of working and business models, and without a vision, transformation efforts can quickly dissolve into a list of confusing and incompatible projects that can lead an organization in the wrong direction. Sharing examples of companies that have not adapted can help bring to life the risks of not changing fast enough.

As with any program, you will need to agree who is going to lead this change within the organization. In a digital change program, cross-functional groups coming together can make all the difference to your success. Real transformation needs to be led from the top. Several new roles have arisen to sit alongside the CEO to support digital transformation efforts, and you might already have some of these in your own organization.

The first new role is the Chief Digital Officer, or CDO. This is usually a senior leader who is focused on driving growth and increasing adoption of digital technologies across the business. Their role would typically be to identify all of the potential areas that can be digitized for better integration, enabling the company to perform more efficiently.

As well as a Chief Digital Officer, you might also hire a Chief Data Officer, a senior executive whose main responsibility is data governance - managing data assets to drive business value, and ensuring compliance over data protection, privacy, and security issues.

A Chief Information Officer, or CIO, has some shared responsibilities with the first two roles, but typically oversees the implementation and strategy of Information Technology. In addition to managing the hardware, software and data that helps other members of the company - from the C-Suite downwards - to do their jobs effectively, the CIO should research new technologies and understand their potential for building value, as well as addressing the risks associated with digital information.

Finally, you might have come across a role called the Digital Transformation Officer, or DTO. This role is essentially to be an internal change agent. They might be a senior leader within the organization who is relieved of their day-to-day duties to drive the transformation program, or they might be brought in externally to give a fresh pair of eyes to existing ways of working. What they must have is the appropriate level of authority to effect change at a senior level, and to be able to inspire others to work in different ways and with different people to bring about transformational change.

Bear in mind that, even as you are transforming for a better tomorrow, you will still need to keep the current business afloat. It is hard managing both the present and future of a business, so most companies are investing in one or more of these new roles to bring their digital transformation vision to life.

Deciding which of these roles you need will depend on the current company structure and the changes to be made, but importantly, none of them will be short-term hires. The digital challenge is only going to get bigger, and these roles need to work hand-in-hand with senior leadership to recognize the issues, align stakeholders and be completely fluent in the language of digital - as well as having the management skills to deal with a lot of internal and external change.

WHAT TO TRANSFORM

So, you have established your digital vision and your leadership team is in place, with everyone in agreement about why you need to transform. Now It is time to work out what you are going to change. This will inform the planning part of your digital transformation strategy, helping you to work out the priority areas that will take you from the present to your digital future.

Based on the findings from your situational analysis, you can work out where you need to make some changes. There are three main areas which companies look to digitally transform: customer experience; creating new business models with new products or services; and modernizing internal and operational processes. Let us start with customer experience, as creating value for your customers should be at the heart of any digital transformation effort.

The first point is to make sure everyone understands what is meant by 'customer experience.' Every point of interaction that customers or users have with your company, whether that is online, offline, directly, indirectly - it all adds up to the customer's experience and how they perceive or feel about your business. You can then gain valuable insights backed by data about this process, and use digital technology to change or improve that experience.

Immersing yourself in your customers' worlds can often help you to understand first-hand what they are doing, how they are feeling, and how you could be doing a better job servicing them. While it might sound obvious, often this is overlooked in our heads-down culture. Conducting focus groups, working as a secret shopper, or even spending time in a call center, on a till or in a delivery van will help you discover very quickly your customers' true needs and frustrations.

A good place to start is by mapping the customer journey, from how and where customers first become aware of your business, to understanding the consideration stages and identifying what pushes them to convert or make a purchase. Today's customer journey is rarely linear, so there might be some areas where digital could be used to add value - by making the journey more seamless, simplifying a process, or reducing issues that regularly occur. Then when you come to mobilize and put your plan into action, you can make these a priority.

Solving problems or pain-points is an effective way of demonstrating results in a digital transformation program - helping to keep staff on board and prove to customers that you are on their side.

Outdoor clothing brand, The North Face, are doing a great job at creating value for their customers. They noticed that the shift towards online ordering has a crucial drawback for some shoppers - what if you want real-time advice on which products are best for you? In an effort to preserve the convenience of an in-store assistant, The North Face are experimenting with Artificial Intelligence, using IBM's Watson and Expert Personal Shopper software. Customers answer questions about their basic details, where they are travelling to, what time of year and what kind of activity they will be doing.

The AI tool will then take that information and leverage big data to recommend the best jacket available - whether It is for commuting daily in Boston, or trekking in Iceland in November, ranked against expected weather, altitudes, and style preference. And of course, as a result of these interactions, The North Face has access to vast amounts of data - not only on who their customers are and what they are buying, but also about the decision-making process before they make a purchase; something which is notoriously difficult to quantify.

On average, visitors spent 40% more time on the site when interacting with the tool, and the 'game-like' approach meant 75% of users said they would use the tool again. By taking advantage of these technological developments, The North Face changed its approach to customer experience, adding value by combining useful product information with an element of entertainment.

Many companies have recognized that the business models they started out with are no longer adequate in the face of the challenges of digital transformation, and they are left with a choice - make a change or get left behind. One industry that has increasingly felt the pressure is retail, with many big-name legacy businesses going bankrupt or simply being overtaken by the competition. Whether It is changing the products and services you offer, or overhauling your business model, sitting still is not an option.

Burberry, the luxury fashion brand, was an early adopter of digital, with its leaders prioritizing digital as a core strategic pillar of the business. Former CEO, Angela Ahrendts realized that weekly traffic to Burberry's online platforms was greater than the number of people visiting all of their retail stores combined. Her priority was to curate a website which would become the hub for the brand's sales, social media, and creative content, removing the limitations of operating solely through brick and mortar stores and transforming Burberry into an eCommerce brand. And they have continued to adapt, unveiling fashion collections on Twitter and Instagram before the styles hit the runway, streaming events live on YouTube and even becoming the first luxury brand to sell through Twitter's "Buy Now" functionality.

Whilst transforming the customer experience or adapting your products and business models are the most visible elements of change, many companies are seeing the benefits of transforming internal processes too. One of the most common changes implemented by businesses is the introduction of agile working. It can be a daunting prospect, especially if you are a global business operating from 1000 offices around the world, but the reality is that thriving in a digital world requires speed and adaptability to stay on top and keep customers happy.

Traditionally, project management processes have followed a 'waterfall approach,' where projects have a pre-defined scope and no opportunity for change after the initial sign-off. As each stage of development is completed, work is passed on to the next relevant department. Agile processes, however, meet the need for faster production times, and allow for continuous improvement, with new iterations made as customer priorities change; so, It is perhaps unsurprising that many companies are rejecting legacy approaches in favor of agile development.

Too often, digital transformation projects are derailed because everything is seen as a priority and there simply are not sufficient resources to do it all. By defining the areas that need to change and prioritizing those changes, you can ensure that the resources you do have are put to the best possible use. This does not mean that your priorities will not change over time - they will! As new technologies are invented or competitors enter the scene, you will need to understand the potential impact, but having a rigorous and well-thought-out plan is the best way to stay on track.

DIGITAL TRANSFORMATION AS HUMAN TRANSFORMATION

The final element that you will need to plan for in your digital transformation strategy is: people. Whilst technology often drives change, delivering that change takes human effort. You could think of digital transformation as human transformation. And to have the talent to transform, you need to have the right culture and the right people in place, with the right skills and mindset.

The truth is, there just are not enough people with the right digital skills to lead the transformation, so organizations need to find ways to address this lack of talent. Rather than focusing efforts on hiring externally, they need to develop the talent internally.

But It is not just a case of upskilling - true transformation requires a shift in attitudes and behaviors, encouraging a shared ethos and new way of working. So, what does this look like in practice?

Collaboration over Competition. Whilst legacy companies may have thrived on competition within departments, the speed of change nowadays means you need people from as many different backgrounds, industries, and teams to work together. Encourage employees struggling with a problem to collaborate and move forward, using mixed age groups and skill-sets so that they can learn from each other and bring different talents to the task at hand. Also think about how you can use technology to aid collaborative work, whether that is through online video conferencing or project management tools. There are hundreds of tools out there, so It is best to focus on those that are simple and multi-functional so that everyone can make use of them.

Be Data-Driven. Nowadays, regardless of your role or job title, you cannot really get away with just having a 'gut feeling' about something - you have to have the data to back it up. Google have found ways of using data not just to improve customer experience, but also for the benefit of their employees. Every year, so-called Googlers fill in the Googlegeist internal survey, covering the major aspects of what a great digital culture should include, from innovation and autonomy, to forward thinking and teamwork. By analyzing the results in detail, Google's leaders can then prioritize areas for improvement going forward.

Digital Transformation is about Recognizing Fear and Embracing Innovation. Individuals broadly fall into one of two groups - those that fear change and might underperform when faced with it, and those that embrace change and thrive within more turbulent environments. When you are expecting teams to do new things with new technologies and processes, you will need to create an environment where fear is both acknowledged and understood. Openness is key, and that needs to be demonstrated by leaders, with everyone speaking the same language. Here are a few tips on building a fear-free culture:

1. Be clear about what you are doing and why - the vision needs to be understood by everyone, so do not be afraid of using success stories to illustrate the changes you want to see.

2. Show that you welcome experimentation, and that problems along the way are to be expected; digital transformation is about learning from failures and moving on!

3. Ensure that you give teams enough time and space to do those experiments, and be empathetic if progress does not happen as quickly as you had hoped. And,

4. Encourage employees to establish processes to help each other, rather than simply following orders in a rules-driven organization. When you need to adapt at speed, you will need your teams to take the initiative.

As part of your digital transformation strategy, you should also look to find the innovators within your business. Remember that group that embraces change? Make the most of what they can offer! You can train for skills gaps, but the ability to see 'beyond the now' is hard to teach on a training program; these people think differently. Often these innovators will be the first to approach leaders with their brilliant ideas, presenting themselves proactively at events or confidently requesting meetings with senior staff. The natural behaviors of these change agents could even motivate others to embrace transformation in ways that are much more powerful than any PowerPoint presentation.

Encourage an Agile Mindset. As more businesses embrace agile workflows, employees have to get used to unfamiliar processes and ways of working. The cross-functional nature and 'group-effort' mentality of agile often requires someone to oversee the various elements. In many businesses, this is the role of a scrum expert, who organizes frequent short meetings with the entire team to check development, progress, and barriers to success. Your scrum expert can also advise on when and how to change direction, if necessary.

By taking people out of their functional silos and putting them in self-managed teams, you are helping to create a new generation of skilled managers who feel empowered to make a difference. Even if you are not ready to embark on a fully agile system, why not start by introducing a few agile principles into the business, like a quick daily stand- up meeting with your team?

The companies that are already thriving in their digital transformation efforts have agile principles at their core, so it will not be too long before those still hanging on to traditional workflow processes find themselves losing traction.

Training. In order to make the most of the talent you have got available, you are probably going to need to invest in some training. There are several different models for upskilling your business, such as setting up an in-house academy, on the job training, real-time feedback, and of course, the kind of online learning you are doing right now!

To really make a difference, you'll need to think about devising the right training plan for the right person; scaling education across geographies and seniority, and adapting the training content as the digital landscape evolves.

Ultimately, a digital transformation strategy is only as good as the organization's ability to execute it. People are critical to the success of the transformation process, and a shortage of talent could be the biggest constraint to true transformation. By developing a culture that encourages a digital mindset, and putting in place a defined learning approach, you have the best chance of transforming successfully.

A PRACTICAL APPROACH TO A DIGITAL TRANSFORMATION

INTRODUCTION

Last time around we explored the aspects of a business that might change as a result of digital transformation, from improving the customer experience to altering your business model, and modernizing internal operations and processes. Now it should be clear that if your transformation is going to be successful, you have to start from within and focus on the people. Today we will look at some of the practical ways of implementing digital transformation and making your vision a reality.

BUILDING AN ENGAGEMENT STRATEGY

Whilst the digital vision for your business might come from one or two senior leaders, to really make transformation happen, you are going to need the support of the whole company. Alongside your overall digital transformation strategy, you should be developing an engagement strategy to make sure the entire organization is committed to the change, and that they are inspired to deliver it.

All too often, change leaders make the mistake of believing that others understand the issues as well as they do, and that they feel compelled to make the same changes. But, of course, that is not always the case.

A big part of your engagement strategy should therefore focus around communication - using multiple channels to get key information and ideas across to everyone in the business. Your engagement strategy should be as carefully planned as any marketing campaign, considering who you are talking to, what the message is and how you are getting it across.

It can be useful to consider some of the reasons a project might fail from a people point of view, and find ways of addressing these in your communications plan. It might be that employees cannot see what is in it for them personally, or perhaps they simply do not understand what is being asked of them. It takes time to get your head around a vision and come to terms with it, and even though you have reached that point, those who are further behind on the journey may need that time too. See if they can articulate the vision back to you - if not, then making it clearer should be your number one priority.

If the issue is getting everyone involved and on board, try finding ways to link business goals to employees' individual goals. You might choose to involve your HR department at this point, as they are often best placed to understand the strengths and skills of staff members, ensuring they can make the best contribution possible.

A transformation project might also suffer if employees do not get the sense that It is a real priority for their managers, or they might feel negatively towards the change if they have been part of a previous initiative that did fail. Digital transformation is one of the biggest changes you can enact. Essentially, you are asking people who have worked in a certain way, sometimes for many years, to change what they know and how they work, and that is hard! Switching to an agile workflow, for example, could have huge benefits, but for some could be perceived as a demotion or removal of status - especially senior employees who have gotten used to being consulted on every decision. Change is often viewed with suspicion and unease, but demonstrating the positive side of digital transformation with small touches and quick wins can have a big impact on behavioral change. For instance, consider showcasing and rewarding someone who has saved time with a new way of working.

It is also worth considering everything else employees are involved in - if they're too busy working on short term goals, they might just not have the mental or physical capacity to focus on longer-term strategies. Similarly, if team members or resources have not been prioritized sufficiently, this can put a real strain on the project itself, as well as staff involvement and morale.

Every one of the issues we have just mentioned is valid, and they can all be addressed through an honest, credible engagement plan. Recruit people onto your engagement team who really care about making a difference, and who have a high level of emotional intelligence. They need to be the kinds of people who can understand what is happening at every level of a business and know where they can make the greatest difference.

How you choose to engage staff internally will depend on the nature of your company and the kind of leaders you have in place, but there are a few methods you could introduce.

Some businesses find presentations to be a good way of engaging employees. This could cover everything from roadshows and showcases to 'lunch and learn' sessions. These face-to-face events should, in some way, make employees feel proud to be a part of this change project, and that their contribution is valuable. You will need to be able to demonstrate transparency about what you are doing and how you are getting buy-in, so think carefully about the story you want to tell.

Awards, shout-outs, and celebrations of success, especially when delivered by senior management, often go a long way in the eyes of employees. You could try making recognition competitive, by running leaderboards for team achievements and shining a light on those who are embracing key elements of the digital transformation vision.

Another way of encouraging engagement in the workplace is through collaboration spaces. These can be online, through internal social media channels, blogs, or newsletters, or they might be physical areas designed for sharing ideas. Wherever you host these spaces or platforms, be clear about their purpose - is it for showing progress, praising accomplishments, or signposting next steps?

The point to remember is that engagement done well is not done remotely - this level of communication requires an element of hands-on work, from either top leaders or engagement teams, supported with information that staff can draw from.

In the most successful transformation efforts, executives use every occasion to re-iterate the digital vision. It is not just about putting on a big display once a year - the vision is built into every presentation; It is woven into performance appraisals and It is central to

all learning and development. Generally, employees want to be more empowered and engaged at work, so make sure you have that positive narrative and that you are taking people with you every step of the way.

TRACKING YOUR PROGRESS

A core part of any strategy is setting out parameters for growth and a clear plan for what you are hoping to achieve. It is not about setting off impulsively with a vague plan to "Be better." You need to work out what success will look like for every aspect of your project, and understand how you are going to measure it. In short, you need a way of seeing if you are on track, and a way of working out how to adapt if you spot any areas for improvement. For this, you will need to set some Key Performance Indicators, or KPIs.

The KPIs you choose will be dependent on what you hope to gain from your digital transformation, which could be anything from increasing revenue, to reducing staff turnover and boosting technology implementation. Every KPI you set should be clearly explained, measurable, achievable, relevant to your goals, and time-dependent, so you can monitor your progress. Working out the best KPIs for your projects can be tricky, but there are a few questions you can ask yourself.

When setting KPIs for transformation, the first question you should ask is: Do your KPIs link back to your vision? By this point, you will have put a lot of effort into justifying and explaining your digital vision, so be sure that every one of your KPIs is going to help you achieve it. This level of focus ensures you are delivering on your promise and will help to stop any other priorities from sneaking in and taking up valuable resources.

The second question is: Are your KPIs actually going to drive success? Good KPIs should keep you focused on the metrics that really matter, reducing the risk of spending time and money on 'vanity metric is such as likes or shares, which are unlikely to have a real business impact. Your KPIs should reflect any changes you are making to the business,

so, if you are experimenting with new channels - like Starbucks' in-app payments or TGI Fridays' order-taking chatbots - you will want to measure the revenue streams that these systems are driving. Of course, new methods might not reach peak efficiency right away, but comparing these new technologies with more traditional operating models can give you a real insight into where your future growth might come from.

The third question is: Have you set people KPIs? Never underestimate how important people are to both a successful business and a successful digital transformation, and setting internal KPIs is a good way of honoring this. Measuring areas like employee satisfaction and average tenure gives employees a voice and demonstrates that they are a valued part of the company.

And finally: Can your KPIs be measured throughout the digital transformation project? Transformation is a journey, and you will need to identify how well you are doing at different stages along the way. You can then use this information to see if a change of direction is needed, and to serve as a useful point of comparison for other digital transformation projects as they launch.

You will need to set benchmarks for your KPIs, based on achievable targets. Benchmarks are vital for informing decision-making during a change program, when multiple initiatives are in play, but they can also be used to help grow other projects and build positive momentum internally.

Some KPIs will be more transitional, and will be replaced as you reach strategic milestones, but others will be constant throughout your transformation. Annual reviews are a thing of the past; it is time to incorporate daily, weekly, and monthly reviews into your overall strategy. Even if the innovation is brand new and you have no idea what KPI to set, have a go and try to link it back to similar channels and products. Remember, you can always change it later!

However, you choose your KPIs, it is vital to have some success criteria in place so you can make the right choices around prioritizing areas for change. As you roll out your transformation initiative, you need to execute and adapt systematically, encouraging a culture of Do, Learn, Grow.

WHAT DOES SUCCESS LOOK LIKE?

So, you have your vision and engagement strategy, and you have set your KPIs. Taking these steps to prepare for change will make a big difference to your success, but the honest truth is that no change program goes completely to plan. People will react in unexpected ways, some of the problems you had anticipated simply will not materialize and crucially, the digital environment will continue to change just as quickly as you can keep up. Effectively managing this constant state of flux requires a different mindset and a willingness to make change happen.

We have said it throughout, but your customers should be at the very heart of your digital transformation strategy. As the ones who will ultimately be buying your product, using your services, and keeping you in business, customer experience is key. Every shift in the market could alter the ways customers behave, and you need to be right there with them, providing solutions they did not even know they needed.

At every stage of your journey, you should be thinking about what your customers might be thinking, feeling, and doing as a result of the changes you are implementing. If you cannot be certain that you are creating value for your customers, you might need to re- prioritize. Of course, there will always be internal and back-end technologies that your customers will not be expressly aware of, but it is good to get into the habit of framing every change in the context of the customer journey. Ultimately, you are asking - how can we make things better for them?

In recent years, McDonald's have answered the request for convenience and an enhanced customer experience with their digital transformation efforts. Thousands of the fast-food chain's restaurants each year are being fitted with touch-screen self-service kiosks and digital menus, allowing customers to place their order in just a few simple steps. McDonald's has removed some of the typical pain-points of traditional in-store purchasing, like waiting in line or risking getting the wrong food when ordering a complicated or customized meal. As a result, purchases made through the kiosks have led to reduced wait-times and an increased average order value of up to 30%, compared to ordering with a cashier.

Digital offers businesses many advantages, and one of those is the quantity of data produced from every single interaction with your customers. Generating data is often the easy part, but knowing how best to collect it, how to interpret it and how to gain valuable insights from data takes a lot more effort.

Disney's Magic Bands are a good example of a company collecting data and using it to its advantage. In an effort to make the theme park experience at Walt Disney World Resort more seamless than ever, guests are provided with a colorful rubber bracelet, fitted with a radio-frequency identification tag. They can use these bands all around the park to pay for meals and merchandise, skip the queues on rides and even unlock their hotel rooms.

The immediate rewards for guests are clear, with everything you need on a single device, but the benefits for Disney are even greater, with real-time hyper-accurate data on what customers buy, where they go, what they eat and which rides they go on. Disney then use this data to better understand their customers and predict buying patterns, to improve targeting options and make the customer experience more personalized. From the logistics side, the data can also be used to ensure the smooth running of the park itself, taking account of particularly busy areas and managing customer service issues accordingly.

Today, the role of data needs to be front and center in all business decisions. Crucially, the data you collect must be treated as a strategic asset, so you will need to make sure you are compliant with all aspects of data protection regulations in the regions you are operating in.

Successful digital transformation strategies think differently about both customers and data, and the Magic Bands are a clear example of how the two areas can benefit each other, providing a great customer experience and the opportunity for Disney to inform its strategies.

But do not forget that your customers are not the only people helping you along your journey - without an engaged and motivated workforce, transformation cannot happen. You need to know whether people are willing and able to make the changes required. Digital transformation is about changing behaviors, and sometimes that means making some tough calls. When staff are used to doing what they have always done, it can take a business-wide shake-up for everyone to understand their new role in this changing world.

As part of their digital transformation, Dutch banking group, ING, re-organized their entire business structure, taking around 3,500 staff members out of traditional silos and coordinating them into nine-person squads, each with a focus of improving productivity and customer satisfaction in an agile operating model. These squads had a mix of IT and commercial team members, with no managers to slow down the process, and were given specific customer experience tasks to perform. Once completed, squads were disbanded and re-formed with a new task.

Alongside the structural change, ING introduced a culture of assessment and reflection, as the learnings from each quarter - both good and bad - were made available to the whole company. And this transformational shift did have a huge impact on the bank's success, going from launching new software releases every few months, to every two weeks, and establishing them as one of the leading mobile banks in the Netherlands.

But it was not an overnight success, and this new way of working came about thanks to a change in focus, led from the top-down; a shift in the way the company viewed successes and failures and, above all, the high percentage of the organization who were willing to embrace agile. By the time the initiative was through, some employees had left the company, but 40% of the existing staff found themselves in a new role at ING, where their skills could be maximized to drive the transformation from within.

Collaboration between teams and departments led ING to success, and if you can use the resources you have in-house to drive digital transformation, that is great! But do not think you have to rely on these.

Digital transformations are often just too specialized for one organization to be able to fully understand and implement. Instead, it is often faster and more cost-effective to partner with another company and work together, than to try and go it alone. You might even think about bringing in your customers to help, encouraging a culture of co-creation and co-innovation.

LEGO, one of the most successful toy companies in the world, was not always in such a strong position. In fact, back in 2004 it was close to bankruptcy, due to poor sales performance and a changing market. Whilst this has signaled the point of no return for some companies, LEGO set out on a new path with a multi-level transformation strategy.

On the product side, they began expanding their business model to include highly lucrative movies and videogames, as well as establishing licensing deals for the likes of Batman, Star Wars and Harry Potter. But on the customer side, they worked out that to get the most engaged users, you have to make them want to be a part of the action!

They built a web-based 3D design tool and encouraged fans to create their own product designs and vote for the creations they wanted to see brought to life. With a self- appointed vision to "inspire and develop the builders of tomorrow," LEGO's decision to partner with its customers did just that - and created an engaged global fan-base at the same time, re-establishing itself as the modern brand it is today.

LEGO's efforts prove that digital transformation does not have to mean a complete overhaul of everything you have ever done. The company has been producing children's toys for nearly 100 years, and still continues to do so. Rather than abandoning their iconic products in favor of an entirely digitized business model, LEGO recognized and embraced the opportunities within digital that would ensure the continued success.

It can be tempting to use digital transformation as a rallying cry to change every aspect of your business. Transforming customer relationships, keeping up with competition, improving employee satisfaction, creating cost efficiencies, and even revitalizing your brand image - all of these areas can fit under the 'digital transformation umbrella.'

But trying to fix everything at once just is not going to work. Instead, the most successful transformations have a logical plan, with each step focused on achievable goals. By separating out key stages, you can demonstrate successes along the way and keep employees engaged. It is also a clear way of ensuring that you are allocating budgets and resources according to priorities, and can cover for any unexpected complications.

Whatever stage you are at with your digital transformation, do not lose sight of the fact that for every organization, It is an ongoing process, not a destination. It takes years of effort to find and nurture the right people, and to learn and apply measures and technologies that can help your business take on the challenge. And of course, just as you are learning and adapting, so too is the industry itself. For many businesses, therefore, digital transformation is not about making a drastic change. Instead, It is about making organizations more adaptive to change, and being able to make appropriate changes when the time is right.

SUMMARY

When the road ahead can seem uncertain at best, It is tempting to put off those difficult decisions - but part of digital transformation is about embracing that fear and channeling it into improving your customers' experiences, pioneering your digital vision, and engaging your workforce. Every company faces a turning point, so now is the time for your own journey. Setting KPIs and goals is a great place to start, and it will help you to prioritize key areas for change and start putting those into action. But before you set off, let us just take a quick look at what we have covered today.

PART II
DIGITAL MARKETING STRATEGY

A HOLISTIC STRATEGY

INTRODUCTION

It is generally accepted that regardless of what you are doing or in what industry, if you want to do it well, you are going to need a carefully planned strategy. And the truth is, It is no different for your digital marketing campaigns. Simply put, a strategy is a roadmap of what you want to achieve, and how you plan to do it, with some measurable goals that allow you to evaluate success. Without a strategy, businesses run the risk of expending unnecessary resources, missing opportunities and being overtaken by the competition.

In this section, we will cover the fundamentals of building a strategy, looking at how to define your goals and KPIs, and the importance of understanding an increasingly complex customer journey.

Thanks to advances in technology and the ways we interact with media, digital marketing has become 'multi-channel.' This means that customers will see your brand in many different places, across a range of platforms and devices. Even these channels themselves can connect and interact, such as when links from a phone-based social media app take visitors to a mobile responsive website.

When thinking about digital, It is important not to have your head stuck in the Cloud, and end up forgetting about more 'traditional' marketing, through media like TV, print, billboards, or events. The online and offline worlds are now so intricately connected - from QR codes in magazines, to GPS software mapping your physical location - that having separate planning efforts for each channel just is not enough anymore. Instead, It is important to create a holistic digital marketing strategy that takes advantage of the specific benefits of each channel individually, and their connected nature.

Many of the fundamental marketing practices that we learn in the 'real world' still apply digitally, and they need to be part of your strategic thinking. No matter where your content is being displayed, you will want to ensure your branding is consistent and your brand identity is recognizable across visual assets like fonts and logos. Given the variety of ways in which customers can interact with your brand, It is vital to ensure that It is being presented consistently across all media, to avoid confusing your visitors or losing that core identity.

The 'voice' that you use in communications also plays a vital role. Whether that is how you describe your products, or how you explain the features and benefits of a particular service, your consumers will want to know that they have come to the right place. Ask yourself: what is unique about your offerings? Why should people buy from you instead of your competitors? Also keep in mind that online visitors tend to have very short attention spans, so alongside having interesting copy, you also need to make your case quickly and concisely, before your potential customers end up getting bored and walking away.

Once you have understood how the fundamentals of marketing fit alongside your brand, It is time to look at the key steps involved in creating a digital marketing strategy.

Step one is situational analysis. One of the most important early steps in developing a strategy is to stop and take a good look at what is already happening in your markets. That way, you will be able to identify where there might be new opportunities, or possible risks. You will also be able to understand the costs and benefits of any changes you are hoping to make. By reviewing the marketplace as a whole, you will be able to gain valuable insights into how your competitors are performing.

But It is not just about what is going on externally. You should also review your own assets, partnerships, capabilities, and gaps in resources. There are a number of well- known models for framing this analysis, including the popular 'SWOT' matrix. Within this framework, you can identify Strengths, Weaknesses, Opportunities or Threats, and they can all be further defined as internal or external, and positive or negative issues.

Data for your situational analysis can be obtained from your current performance metrics if you are already engaged in digital marketing. Some key focus areas might be: the strength of your online brand, the number of email subscribers you have, or even some known issues with your conversion rates. You can also gain sales intelligence from your CRM, or Customer Relationship Management system, or from talking to existing customers - a tactic, which is commonly overlooked, but which can be a highly valuable source of information.

And finally, you can better plan for how to implement new digital strategies if you understand your business's current status, so you should be assessing your organizational structure, and your personnel and technology capabilities, and keep them in mind as you progress.

If done well, situational analysis is a valuable reality check on your digital marketing activities and plans. It is an important part of your strategic planning, and It is also worth reviewing on at least an annual basis to ensure you are still on track, or to make any additions or adjustments.

SETTING GOALS AND OBJECTIVES

Most businesses, big or small, will have a strategic plan that sets out their overall objectives. These are usually expressed at a very high level and are usually fairly vague. Often, these are associated with making money, but you might have a few secondary objectives such as social entrepreneurship, growing your target audience, or nurturing customer loyalty. Your digital marketing plan, therefore, is what sets out the strategic goals, tactics and measures of success that will support your business objectives.

If an objective is a high-level statement of what you want to achieve overall, then your goals describe the steps needed to reach these objectives. They are expressed using terms such as "Increase...," "Reduce..." or "Identify...," and they should give clear directions to develop your marketing tactics. There are all sorts of models and frameworks for describing effective goals, but essentially, they are all making the same point - that you cannot just choose goals for the sake of it, and your goals must be thought out in order to achieve success.

When setting your goals, there are a few key questions you can ask yourself to ensure you are hitting the mark:

Is your goal realistic for your business to achieve? You can use the data from your situational analysis to understand if you already have the resources, skills, and budget to make it happen; and It is also worth figuring out if this is a short-term goal, or if it might take a little longer to get there.

Is your goal well-defined? By this we mean - can everyone who has a role in achieving it, understand and readily explain what is involved? If the goal is too complicated for your staff to grasp, they will not be able to work with it.

Is your goal defined in a way that makes it simple to evaluate progress? In order to analyze success, your goals will need to be measurable, and that can be easier for some than others. Measuring if you have successfully increased revenue is fairly simple, but goals such as increasing brand awareness can be tougher to judge. Be sure to agree a measurement strategy before you start, so you do not get any nasty surprises later on.

Finally, if you reach your goal, will the outcome proactively help your business? This is why It is so important to match your goals to your objectives. If your overall objective is to increase revenue, setting a goal to increase your Facebook followers might not be much help at all, so you will need to look for something more directly relevant.

However, you decide on your goals, they should be there to help you achieve your business objectives, by making it really clear what you are working towards, how you will know when you get there, and the timeframe within which you are working. If you find you have ended up with a large number of goals, try to work out the most important and pressing issues, and maybe add a brief justification for the inclusion of each goal, based on your current situation.

Once you have decided on your goals, the next step in your strategy is to define a measurable target for each one. By adding parameters for success, you can then identify when you have reached your goal. Without a target… goals are essentially meaningless.

One mistake made by a lot of marketers is to concentrate on tactics that aim for immediate sales. Whilst this is understandable, it does not consider that very few of your online visitors are ready to buy at all times. Even some top eCommerce sites

still have conversion rates below 5%. Instead, you can build your strategy to include a balanced mix of activities in three areas:

Acquisition: These are tactics aimed at attracting new visitors to your digital presence. An acquisition goal might be: 'Increase web traffic by 10,000 visitors in the next quarter'.

Then there's Behavior: This covers all of the interactions that visitors have with you, other than actual purchases and conversions, so a useful behavior goal could be: 'Increase shares of social media content by 3,000'.

And finally, Conversion: This is where you motivate visitors to fulfill your desired outcomes. Whilst this can mean purchases, conversions also include newsletter sign-ups or submitting a lead form. Sticking with the objective of making money, a valuable conversion goal could be: 'Increase average order value to over $50'.

By ensuring that you create one or two goals in each of these areas, you will cover a broad range of marketing strategies - from making sure people hear about your brand; to engaging them with content, resources, and expertise; and finally, persuading them to act.

Going one step further beyond objectives and goals, we have KPIs or 'Key Performance Indicators.' These are metrics which help you to evaluate your progress against your goals. Because they are a way of measuring something, KPIs are always represented as numbers - whether It is a total count, an average, a percentage, or a ratio.

Each KPI that you establish is associated with one of your goals, so you should be working with a finite number of KPIs at any one time. In defining your KPIs, you need to think carefully about which metrics would be most useful in measuring your success around that particular goal, and whether they will provide insights that you can act

on to improve. KPIs are only worthwhile if they make a difference to your business understanding and give you actionable insights. Otherwise, they are just 'feel-good' numbers.

Albert wants to increase visitor engagement with his website, so he is trying to find the right KPIs. One of the most popular KPIs used is 'Average bounce rate,' but in most cases, It is not actually that useful. Measuring the bounce rate will tell Albert how many people left his website without making a second click, but it will not give him any real insight into why this is happening. In order to make any real changes, he will have to dig a little deeper.

Albert could choose page views as a Key Performance Indicator. This can give some information, but it still leaves a lot of unanswered questions. If Albert's page views are high, does it mean that his visitors loved his content? Or does it mean that they had to look in lots of places before they could find what they wanted? Further analytics research can help in this situation, but we still have not found the right KPI for Albert's goal of increasing engagement.

What about 'visitor loyalty,' then? Actually, this one could be very helpful indeed, as it looks at how often visitors are returning to Albert's site. High loyalty rates, either from returning visitors, or those who advocate or convert again are really positive results. If Albert has some lower loyalty levels appearing in his analytics reports, then he can combine that with data about what visitors were looking for and which pages they did visit, to plan some much-needed improvements around his site.

As part of your strategy, you will also need to think about the most useful way to express goals, targets and KPIs. Which is more helpful - a simple number, a percentage, or a ratio, and what does each one tells you? Will you learn more from studying your measurements as values, or is it better to look at the percentage increase or decrease? Remember that for clarity, each KPI should only correspond to one metric.

By working with only one or two KPIs per goal at any one time, you can focus your efforts on deriving usable and meaningful data, rather than risking an information overload. If a KPI is no longer useful or relevant, It is time to reassess and replace it with something that is better for your current status.

THE CUSTOMER JOURNEY

As technologies and platforms evolve, so too do our expectations as customers. Nowadays, personalization and customization are becoming increasingly powerful components of online success. In order to do these effectively, you need to build an in- depth understanding of your customers and prospects; learning who they are, what they like, how they communicate, what problems they have that you could solve, and of course, how they experience doing business with you.

One way of doing this is by creating personas. Personas are fictitious profiles that bring the characteristics of your target customers to life, to help you plan your interactions with them, and understand their typical needs, behaviors and preferred communication platforms and styles. Ideally, you should develop a number of different personas to reflect the various segments of your markets, and to give you a wider view of your marketing requirements. It can be helpful to name these personas in order to keep them easily identifiable and separate from each other.

Well-defined personas will take everything into consideration - from customer demographics to familiarity with your business - and it can feel a little overwhelming. Depending on the type of company, the focus could be slightly different, with B2B companies looking at 'professional' attributes like job title and education, whereas B2C companies can gain more insight from more 'personal' data like interests and marital status.

To make it all feel more practical, let us think about some of the personas that a brand of running shoes might develop...

At the most basic level, you should understand the age, gender, and geographical location of your audience, as well as the languages they speak. So, we have A, a 25-year old male from Texas; B, a 16-year old female from France; and C, a 32-year old male from Canada. Already, there is quite a lot of variation across this international brand's customers, so we will need to define the personas a little more.

The next step then, is understanding why customers are coming to your business and what they expect to find. One of our shoe buyers may have a limited budget, and so is not looking for detailed reviews or information, but just wants to filter the lowest price models. Perhaps another persona type is an aspiring athlete and therefore wants to test out a range of models and benefit from expert recommendations. And our third persona wants a comfortable, but stylish shoe for running around with their children, so is interested in the various colors and styles available.

Now that you have an idea of who your audiences are and what they want, how do you know where to reach them? Customers are so used to being able to find what they want across platforms and sites, that if you are not providing for them, they will simply go elsewhere. As part of your strategy, you will need to understand your customers' buying preferences, considering if one prefers to shop in store, another favors desktop computers, and if the third is more content to make purchases through their mobile device. Using these insights and developing rich characteristics about each of your personas means you can successfully tailor your strategy, and communicate to each potential customer in more relevant ways.

Because different areas of your business will have varying perspectives on your customers, personas are best developed by teams across the organization. Include a range of opinions from marketing, sales, and customer service, as well as higher-level management if possible. You should also be using external research sources such as social media, online forums, and customer interviews, comparing your ideal profiles with your actual customers as you go.

In addition to defining your personas, It is also important to recognize that customers have different mindsets, depending on where they are along the path to purchase. They may have only just heard of your brand, or maybe they are a loyal customer that you want to concentrate on keeping.

Due to multiple touch-points and decisions, working out exactly how customers reach the point of purchase is a constant struggle for marketers, but broadly speaking, the stages of the buying cycle are fairly standard.

Whether It is your first sale, or your thousandth, it often starts with awareness and intent. Customers are quick to identify a need, but they might not currently know about your business, or that your products or services could be just what they are looking for. This is where you need to make your prospects aware that you are there, and engage them in what you have to offer.

Now the customer knows about you, they have moved into the consideration stage - but that means they are probably also researching other options and comparing solutions and prices. At this stage, you need to understand their behaviors, and convince them that your business is the right choice.

Moving on, and we have made it! The customer is at the decision stage, and they are ready to buy from you! Now It is important to make that process as painless as possible, and to deal with anything that might get in the way of a completed transaction.

Last, but certainly not least, come retention and advocacy. Most companies aim for repeat business from their customers, so after the initial purchase, you can focus on customer satisfaction, loyalty, and beginning the cycle again. Importantly, customers can join the buying cycle at any stage, whether they are an existing customer stocking up on their favorite items, or a potential customer with no prior knowledge of your brand, so providing for every eventuality is vital.

When marketers talk about 'the customer journey,' they are referring to all of the experiences that a customer has with you, through the duration of your business relationship. While this can be hard to track over time, customer journey mapping is a way of documenting these experiences, and understanding what the customer does and where those actions take place.

The map should be completed with one of your personas in mind. Start by making a list of all of the touchpoints where that customer might interact with you at each stage of the buying cycle, as well as the methods and channels they might use.

Where the customer journey actually begins will depend on whether you are looking at a new or existing customer. Marie is happy with her current brand of running shoes, and sees a magazine advertisement for a new model of shoes from the same manufacturer. This starts her buying cycle at the retention stage. As a follow-up to the print campaign, Marie receives an email from the seller, with offers on the latest designs, bringing her to the awareness stage. Next up is the consideration stage, which is often a little longer, as Marie goes to the manufacturer's website to review styles and specifications. She might also visit a range of online forums and review sites, or she might turn to social media to research other users' opinions, or to find price comparisons.

Once Marie has narrowed it down, she goes along to the manufacturer's store to try out the running shoes she is chosen. Happy with her choice, she purchases the shoes in-store. Often, for marketers, decision is not the last stage in the cycle, and It is not the case here either. We are actually back to retention again, as Marie receives another email from the manufacturer, this time checking that she is satisfied with her new purchase, and even providing some after- care tips. At this point, Marie becomes an advocate of the brand. She goes on to write a review on the store website, tweet about her experience and recommend both the shoes and the brand to her friends, starting the awareness stage of a new cycle.

Understanding the customer journey is a vital step in any campaign strategy, but mapping the buying cycle across various potential touch-points can give helpful insights for working out which types of content to produce, and where to host it for maximum impact.

THE DIGITAL CHANNELS

If the first steps in building an effective digital marketing strategy are setting goals and defining your target audiences, then the logical next step is using those insights to define the specific channels you will use to implement that strategy.

It is not just a one-size-fits-all approach when it comes to digital channels, and there is a lot to take into consideration, from tactics and expected outcomes, to budgets and resources. And all the way along, you need to ask whether each channel is actually going to help with what you are trying to achieve. In this chapter, we are going to set up a framework for determining the best channels for three key areas of business goals - Acquisition, Behavior and Conversion.

ACQUISITION

Most companies will have a dedicated strategy for acquisition, or how you intend to attract visitors and drive traffic to your website, social media platforms or mobile

app at the initial stages of the buying cycle. Although 'number of visitors' is a popular dashboard metric for some executives, just trying to obtain as much traffic as possible will not necessarily help you to achieve your goals. It is actually more a case of quality over quantity, with most businesses focusing on acquiring qualified visitors who fit the profile of their ideal customers, and are more likely to engage and, ultimately, convert.

Since acquisition focuses on attracting traffic, the goals used to achieve this often address either increasing brand awareness - because improved awareness increases the likelihood that people will search for your business - or they focus on reducing the cost of using paid media to gain these new visitors. But successful marketing strategies are not just about selecting goals that sound useful; you need to really understand how these goals will help you achieve your specific objectives, and what it is you need to measure. In order to see what this means in practice; we are going to follow the marketing strategy of a brand of headphones...

This is Claire, she works as Strategic Director for 'EasyListening,' a large international brand of headphones. As an already established business, she is hoping to increase awareness of her brand across a younger target audience, so she might start looking at the number of branded keywords used in the searches that are currently bringing visitors to her website and social media pages.

It might also be worth Claire understanding her brand's share of search, to help with her goal of acquisition. Share of search refers to how often a website appears in organic search results for specific keywords. This means she can take the keywords her visitors are actually using in their search queries, and match her search strategy to them.

Another goal which directly relates to acquisition is increasing the Click-Through Rate, which refers to the number of people who click on a link to your website or social media. These links can appear pretty much anywhere, from paid and organic search results, to email newsletters, social postings, and even mobile messaging. If Claire can understand where most of her traffic is coming from, she can work out where to invest her budget in the future.

Finally, Claire might also set a goal to increase the number of quality backlinks, or hyperlinks posted by relevant influencers or shared on social media, linking back to her brand's website. Backlinks are particularly useful for boosting SEO rankings, and increasing the chance of a site being found.

Setting hundreds of goals for every aspect of your digital marketing activity means you will not have the scope or ability to really assess what is working and what is not. By tailoring your goals to your objectives, and selecting a few to focus on, you will have a much better view of your business needs at any particular time.

When working with an acquisition goal of driving traffic to your digital presence, selecting the channels you will focus on should not be a snap decision. Instead, they should be based on the findings of your analytics reviews, persona definitions and customer mapping, and the resources and budgets you have available. It is also useful to look at what you already know or have in place. Which channels currently drive the most traffic? Of those, can you tell which ones send the most qualified visitors which could help you achieve your desired outcomes?

In selecting and prioritizing your channels, remember that within this framework, we are currently only thinking about the use of each channel with regards to acquisition. Always ask yourself - will this channel attract traffic to my digital presence? What that traffic actually does and where it goes afterwards, is outside of this scope.

Traditionally, marketing activity on these channels has been divided into the three categories of paid, owned and earned media, and It is important to understand the benefits and drawbacks of each.

Paid advertising on third party sites is a key tool for attracting visitors, and it has the advantage of being comparatively quick to implement. You could also consider sponsoring links in the email newsletters of partners and compatible businesses that are likely to have audiences within your target market. As with our headphone brand, acquisition is all about getting your name in the right places, so the right people can find you. If you are an eCommerce company, you might already have relationships with affiliates or distributors, who could refer traffic to you in return for commissions or discounts.

On the owned side, your website and blog posts should contain keywords and content optimized for SEO purposes, which should hopefully generate those all-important links from other recognized sites. If you have a database of active subscribers, you will have access to the addresses and phone numbers of users who have already agreed to receive your messages. These users, therefore, are more likely to be responsive to your content, and to click through to your other digital assets.

Earned media is certainly worthwhile, but it can require a little more effort in terms of the strategic placement of your content, such as articles, videos, and press releases, on third party sites. Here, the focus is encouraging public relations coverage, backlinks to direct visitors to your site, and to attract influencers who can help you in the long-term.

The major channels for acquisition are usually search (a combination of paid and organic), email and mobile marketing. Social media and display advertising are typically not as effective for this purpose because they tend to generate fewer, and less qualified, visitors. The combination of channels you choose will vary depending on your overall goals, but it will also vary according to how you put them to use.

If EasyListening wants to make the most of search as a channel for driving both new and existing traffic to its digital presence, it will need to work on its keyword strategies. It is not just a case of opting for or bidding on keywords that you think might work. Instead, It is about really understanding which are the words and phrases that customers actually use to describe your products and services, and optimizing against those. In the case of tech products like headphones, Claire must make sure she is not losing out on traffic by using over-complicated jargon.

Let us say EasyListening decides to run an advertising campaign to boost acquisition. Retargeting, or remarketing can be a very effective option if done well. But it can be hard to strike the balance of reminding consumers of products they may have already viewed, without seeming overbearing or invasive. Setting frequency caps on how often a single user sees an ad is a good way around this. Remember, you are trying to drive traffic to the site, not away from it. For all forms of advertising, It is important to watch your return on investment carefully. It can be all too easy to let campaigns run automatically, without having a clear understanding of what you are spending, and what you are getting back.

We mentioned that by using your blog to promote and display your owned content, and hosting it on your website, you can create a central hub for visitors. As you assess your acquisition strategy, make sure that every channel is fully integrated with the blog, and that you have a plan for leveraging your content as far as possible. For example, it might be worth seeing if there is an SEO optimization template for blog postings, or if you can notify appropriate influencers of relevant new content, or share it on social media.

Speaking of influencers, remember that they are people too! In the same way you might create personas for target audiences, you can define personas for key influencer types, and match these to the audiences you are trying to reach. Although the one-to-one nature of influencer relationships makes it a longer-term strategy, if you can carefully plan who to approach, how to do so, how often and what types of content to offer, backlinks and suggestions from well-known influencers can be a valuable tool for achieving your acquisition goals.

When defining your acquisition strategies, It is good to bear in mind that certain activities will take longer to achieve the desired results, so setting both short- and long-term goals is important. The optimal way to acquire consistent traffic is through your existing email or mobile subscriber database, or through social media followers who are already engaged with your content and could refer you to others. For short-term wins, paid media can be implemented quickly, and is effective at increasing your visibility, but it should always be monitored to make sure that the visitors you are attracting are the right ones!

A well-thought out acquisition plan will aim to move towards the longer-term, higher- quality channels that produce the best results, according to the goals you set in the early planning stages of your campaign.

BEHAVIOR

If acquisition goals are all about driving traffic to your digital presence, then behavior goals are about what visitors do when they arrive. The behavior section of your holistic digital marketing strategy deals with everything that you want visitors to do around

your campaign, other than specifically completing a transaction. This could be anything from following you, to sharing your content or writing a review. Behavior covers the consideration stages of the buying cycle, where customers are researching further before making any decisions, and it relates to both new and existing customers.

Given that the vast majority of your visitors will not be ready to make an immediate purchase, understanding how your marketing affects them at this stage can give real insights into how to engage with users, how to convince them of your credibility and value, and hopefully, how to keep them coming back to your digital properties.

The key activity in your behavioral strategies will be producing valuable and entertaining content that will be liked, shared, and talked about, so your goals in this section should focus on measuring engagement and reach. But with that in mind, you will need to consider what is realistic for your business, in terms of how often visitors should return, and why. News sites, for example, might expect readers to consume content every day, whilst eCommerce sites might want customers to return on a weekly basis.

So, EasyListening has successfully driven lots of new, qualified traffic to its website, but now needs to focus on its behavior strategy. An effective goal could be increasing depth of engagement with the content on its website. Claire could just look at the amount of time users spend on the site, but that does not guarantee that they are actually reading her content. Instead, she could study which pages are the most popular with certain visitors, and look for any patterns in the types of content they engage with.

Increasing visitor loyalty might seem like an obvious goal, but it can often get overlooked. Frequency and recency reports provide information about how often visitors return to a site, and how much time has passed since a user's last visit. It can be useful to map this to EasyListening's content strategies, and if Claire is trying to encourage repeat visits, she should make sure there is enough new content there to bring visitors back.

As most businesses' behavior strategies will focus on interactions with their content, 'increasing social sharing for maximum reach and visibility,' as well as 'increasing positivity around campaigns and content,' are all common goals. Followers, likes, comments and reviews do not necessarily contribute to your bottom line, but they can be a good indicator of engagement, and a step in the right direction in the buying cycle. One way of increasing engagement could be through encouraging EasyListening's customers to create their own user-generated content, in the form of blogs, shared photos and hashtags. Although, it is always worth keeping an eye on the amount and quality of the content you receive.

If you are encouraging your customers to be vocal, make sure you have a contingency plan in case you do not like what they are saying. Setting up support services to deal with complaints can go a long way to boosting customer satisfaction levels.

As with acquisition, channel selection for your behavior strategy should be based on a review of your personas, customer journeys and your current performance. Think about the channels where your visitors are likely to consume the most content. Is your content better received, and shared more in some channels than others? Do your various personas consume content differently, and how will you manage this?

As with acquisition strategies, your blog and website still play an important role in your behavior plans. After all, if you have spent a lot of time and effort driving traffic to your site, now It is about giving them a reason to stay. Your website can also host important customer service content, such as knowledge bases, frequently asked questions, and even live chat functions. If you are running email marketing campaigns, using CRM data to create more personalized messaging can also help to nurture relationships with both potential and existing customers. And after all, if the content feels more relevant to your customers, they are more likely to continue to engage.

Beyond your owned media, It is becoming increasingly less likely that your content will appear in social media news feeds, unless you pay to promote it. This makes earned media an even more important factor, as reviews and influencer mention - across your site and on third parties - can both enhance your credibility and increase the impact of your product whilst customers are at the consideration stage of the buying cycle.

If you decide to run an ad campaign, It is important to think about what content to promote and where. Social media advertising, for example, allows for very granular targeting, so you can use your personas to create audience profiles and carefully monitor results. Of course, not all of your customers will use all social media platforms. Tailoring the content and spaces to your audience, alongside dynamic landing pages and messaging activities are keyways of increasing personalization, and the relative success of your campaign. If EasyListening is looking to engage a younger audience, then investing in platforms like Facebook or Snapchat might be a good way to go.

One way of understanding how far to go with personalization is through plotting empathy maps. By predicting what your personas might think, feel, say, and do, you can get an idea of what they might appreciate, and what could put them off. For example, sending multiple retargeting emails to a customer who only visited once may not be the best approach. Thinking specifically about behavior, remember that you are looking to provide value in your messages, with a goal of maintaining customer satisfaction and awareness, rather than just focusing on click-throughs.

Once you have identified the spaces in which online conversations are taking place, knowing when you, as a brand, should get involved is another issue. As part of your strategy, you will need to think about the voice of your brand across social media platforms. This relates to the consistency of your brand and message, but also to the more logistical elements, like who will write the posts and where they will appear. This is often a resourcing issue, as different sized companies will have varying takes on how many staff handle their channels, and whether they have multiple accounts for different regions or target audiences. You will need to match your social media strategies to the scope and scale of your business, and ensure there are clear policies in place to govern online conduct by employees.

It is natural to concentrate on acquiring and converting traffic, which can be easily measured and which often produce more tangible results. But as we have seen, behavior strategies are a necessary step to guiding customers to the point of conversion, as this stage encompasses the majority of your interactions with visitors. Make sure that you evaluate success and that you can prove the return on your investment in these activities, so that they continue to receive attention and resources.

CONVERSION

The final aspect of our holistic digital marketing strategy is conversion, which focuses on a company's ability to persuade customers to fulfil a set of desired outcomes, such as generating direct revenue, and other business goals, like new leads and newsletter sign-ups. Having nurtured prospects along the customer journey to this point, you will want to avoid any friction or issues that could change their mind in the final decision-making moment. Even today, around 75% of online shopping carts are abandoned, so this still represents a significant challenge.

At this stage of your digital marketing planning, It is important to identify all of the various calls to action across your website and wider content, so that you are aware of every outcome that you are looking for, and to enable you to optimize performance for each one. These include both macro-conversions, which are usually purchases, bookings or registrations, and micro-conversions, which consist of smaller steps such as lead submissions, subscriptions, and account creation.

When setting conversion goals, a common mistake is to focus only on actual conversions and immediate revenue. Ideally, you should also consider some longer- term business development and profit goals. Typical goals for a conversion strategy include, fairly obviously, increasing the conversion rate of every call to action, and increasing the average order value. This last point refers to the average amount spent in each eCommerce transaction, and is often achieved through upselling or cross-selling, offering alternative or additional products as customers are checking out. Just measuring incoming revenue gives you some idea, but knowing how much individual customers usually spend means you can focus your strategies and see where you might be missing out. One key issue around eCommerce purchases is the high rate of abandoned shopping carts, so in order to reduce this, you will need to identify any obstacles or issues that deter customers from completing transactions, and test out some solutions.

You might also look to increase your lifetime customer value, focusing on the long-term relationship you have with your customers, or perhaps set a goal to reduce your cost per acquisition. In order to calculate your final return on investment, you will need to factor in all of the costs involved in acquiring each customer.

Remember that here, we are only focusing on making the conversion process as friction- free and compelling as possible, so it can be useful to plan for the types of content, media and communication styles that might motivate customers to purchase. Where are the optimal places for your calls to action, and how can you phrase offers and promotions to be the most appealing?

Another important question when reviewing your customer journeys in the last stages of the buying cycle is the relationship between online and offline behavior. Do your customers typically research online and buy in-store? Or is it the other way around? Either way, you will want to ensure the channels you use are well-integrated so that customers can move seamlessly from one to the next.

If you are focusing on a paid media approach, then retargeting display and social media ads can be effective methods of reconnecting with customers, either to remind them of products they might have viewed, to persuade them to check out an abandoned cart, or to suggest more suitable alternatives.

In your owned media strategy, It is important that your purchase set-up is effective for when and where customers are ready to buy, such as using a mobile device. If you do need to appeal to your customers in-store, it might be worth exploring beacon technology, whereby users with your mobile app can be sent relevant offers, or even reminded of an item in their mobile shopping cart.

When choosing the best channels and spaces for your conversion strategy, bear in mind that if a customer is going to part with their money, they have to feel comfortable and content to do so. For example, using paid media for retargeting can be effective, but there is a fine line between reminding prospects about your offerings, and making them feel like you are invading their privacy. Apply both knowledge of your customers and careful testing to establish optimal frequency caps, so that your ads give customers the final push in the right direction, rather than pushing them away.

It is also important to identify and minimize any last-minute conversion issues that might either get in your customers' way, or put them off entirely. These could be anything from unexpected shipping costs, to asking too many questions on a sign-up form. Since analytics cannot tell you why a customer did not complete a transaction, brief online surveys or email messages can be helpful in gathering feedback.

Once the conversion has taken place, personalization becomes more important than ever. Customers want to feel appreciated, and this sentiment can go some way to encouraging repeat purchases or positive reviews. Your CRM systems can help to define appropriate customization for each consumer, so be sure to follow up purchases with either a thank you email, or with some relevant product tips or advice.

Because of its singular focus, the conversion section of your digital marketing strategy might seem less complex than the acquisition or behavior areas, but it is no less important. Often, It is harder to ascertain exactly why customers act in a specific way at this stage, as there are a number of factors in play. For this reason, continually testing and optimizing your strategy is as important as having a solid plan to start with.

A BUDGET FOR OUR STRATEGY

Once you have set your digital marketing goals, defined your targets, and your channels have been selected and prioritized, It is time to move on to implementation. In order to do this, you will need to establish a budget, and decide how to allocate spending across your chosen channels. As part of the review process, you should also have decided what you can do in-house, and what you might have to outsource. In this chapter, we will take you through some of the key considerations of putting a digital marketing strategy into practice.

BUDGETS AND AGENCY BRIEFS

For many marketers who might be more comfortable with words than numbers, the prospect of setting a budget can be a little overwhelming. That is why many marketing managers admit to not fully understanding the impact that a change in the budget could have on their company's results.

Having a clear view of how your expenses correlate to your marketing successes makes a big difference to your strategy. If you cannot justify the resources you are requesting, or you cannot explain how a small increase in your budget might increase overall business profits, you are unlikely to get what you ask for.

When creating budgets, there are a few considerations to keep in mind:

First of all, follow the 'ABC' framework, and plan your budgets around your acquisition, behavior, and conversion goals. It can be very tempting to spend disproportionate amounts of your budget in one area - especially if it looks like it will provide a quick win, like paid media or conversion mechanisms. But the whole point of a holistic digital marketing strategy is taking all aspects of the customer once journey and the buying cycle into account, so you should aim to allocate your resources in a way that supports all of your tactics appropriately.

It can also be helpful to align your spending with your goals and timeframes. Many companies have difficulty in deciding how much to spend on marketing. Of course, this will be different for every business, but a lot depends on whether you are already established or new to the market, and how quickly you need to see results. New companies are likely to spend more to gain initial visibility, and to use paid tactics that can generate a quicker return than say, earned media.

Understanding the integration of your channels is a key factor in deciding how to spend your budget. Across your strategy, there are a number of opportunities to take advantage of the interplay between various marketing channels, and this also applies to budgeting and calculating the value of your spending, as some channels will influence the results that you have in others. For example, an inspiring or informative social media posting might be a factor in increasing final conversion rates. If you do not take insights like these into account when allocating resources and evaluating results, you could end up overspending in one area, or ignoring a potentially successful avenue.

Finally, remember to consider hidden costs. Although It is much easier to calculate return on actual money spent, bear in mind that for a complete picture of your marketing value, you need to include all of your other expenses that helped you get there. That is equipment, software, design, and development and, of course, employee costs.

In order to maximize the effectiveness of your marketing budget and strategic planning process, there are some important metrics that you will need to understand.

Cost per Acquisition (CPA) is the total of what it costs your business to acquire a new customer, and It is usually expressed as your marketing costs, divided by the number of customers. So, if you spend $1000 on a marketing campaign and acquire 100 visitors, but only 20 of them make a purchase, then your CPA for actual customers is $50.

Allowable Cost per Acquisition (ACPA) takes CPA a step further, and represents the maximum that you can afford to spend to acquire a customer.

This is calculated as:

Total revenue, minus all of your expenses, including production, fulfilment, and profit- taking. For example, imagine your product sells at $100. Your production costs to make it are $45, other operations are $25 and your minimum required profit is $20. In other words, if you spend any more than $10 marketing this product, you would risk losing money.

Return on Ad Spend (ROAS) is a useful metric for understanding how successful your paid media spending is. It is calculated by dividing your revenue from advertising sources by the cost of that advertising. Simply put, if your ads cost $100, but your customers spend $1000 as a result of the ads, then your Return on Ad Spend is $10.

Return on Investment is a measure of the profit or loss earned from an investment. To work this out, you can write out your total profit or return, minus your total costs on the investment, and divide all that by your total costs again. ROI is typically expressed as a percentage, so multiply your result by 100.

Finally, you might want to consider the Lifetime Customer Value. As it sounds, this is the revenue that you are likely to generate over the total relationship with a customer. There are a number of ways of calculating this, but in simple terms, it can be expressed as your average order value, multiplied by the average number of orders. For example, if your product sells for $100 and the average customer buys 10 of them over their lifetime, then you are looking at a lifetime customer value of $1,000.

As part of your company reviews and analyses, it should have become clear whether or not you need to outsource certain responsibilities, rather than trying to do everything in-house. Agencies naturally bring reliable expertise and resources, and can be a great option for all kinds of businesses. Once you

've selected the agency that you would like to work with, whether It is for advertising, content creation, or development of mobile apps or games, you will need to give them a very comprehensive idea of what you are looking for from the campaigns that they will run for you. The quality of the brief that you provide will have a significant impact on the quality of work that the agency performs, and potentially on the cost of the process. The more you can tell them about your needs, the better the understanding will be of the expectations on both sides.

Under the holistic digital marketing plan that you have created, you can provide your agency with some detailed information on the following key areas:

First up, your goals and targets. It is important for all parties involved to be on the same page about what you are trying to achieve, and which channels you have selected and prioritized.

It is also important to be clear on your measures of success. Understanding your KPIs and associated targets will give your agency a clear picture of how you will assess the progress of the campaigns that they are responsible for. This also shows how you will evaluate the agency, and gives them a chance to highlight any areas where your expectations or time- frames might be unrealistic.

Finally, do not be afraid to be upfront about your ideas for creative. Based on the customer personas and research that you have included in your plan, you should already have some ideas about the types of content, media, and messaging that your target markets will respond to best. This will, in turn, help the agency to produce initial designs that are more suited to your thinking, rather than risking endless conversations back and forth.

In addition to providing the agency with your strategic digital marketing plan, you will also need to create a written brief for their services. Putting your brief in writing, rather than relying on verbal instructions, allows your requirements to be widely shared, and it documents your expectations and measures of success. That way, everyone involved should have a clear understanding and can question any ambiguities. The brief should be seen as a form of contract, and treated with the same level of respect.

Having said that, a good brief should usually live up to its name, and be restricted to one or two pages, alongside any background material, such as persona and customer mapping research. The brief is designed to clarify your objectives, provide necessary information and most importantly, inspire agency personnel in their creative process.

One essential component of an effective brief is being clear on your high-level objective. Before jumping into the specific campaigns that you want an agency to run, It is helpful to give the bigger picture about what is going on in your business and markets, and why you have chosen this particular route. Maybe there are new opportunities in the marketplace that you are looking to capitalize on, or potential issues you are looking to get ahead of.

Now's the time for campaign-specific details, in the main part of the brief. These should include your goals, targets and KPIs for the campaign, and the impact you hope it will have. Be sure to include any insights about your customer demographics and media consumption preferences, as well as any creative elements that must be included or excluded. You might also want to say something about the campaign messaging, tone of voice, consistency of branding and how the features and benefits will be communicated. Approaches differ as to how much detail to include. Some companies like to offer as much direction as possible, whilst others prefer to rely on the creative instincts of the agency - finding what works for your business is up to you!

The final part of the brief covers administrative details such as key dates, project milestones and timings, budgeting, specific evaluation criteria for the agency and a confirmed approval process, including the names of all stakeholders and authorized signatories. You should clearly define the role and responsibilities of both sides - those that you will undertake, and those that you expect the agency to fulfil.

Along with a written brief, It is important to kick things off with an in-person meeting, in which you can provide more stories and detail about your overall objectives and hopes for each campaign. This provides further input about the background and your intended emotional appeal, and allows for questions and a deeper understanding of the project on both sides.

It should be evident from the information needed to brief an agency, just how vital having a clear digital marketing strategy is for today's businesses. And, as useful as this strategy is internally, if you decide that you need external help to implement your tactics, then the quality of your strategic research and planning will directly relate to the quality of your briefings, and to the additional effort needed to create them.

ANALYTICS AND MEASURING SUCCESS

So, now you have written your strategic marketing plan, and successfully briefed your employees and agencies on implementing it - how do you know if you are actually getting the results you hoped for? You will need to make sure you have a system in place for measuring success, and that you fully understand the implications of, and uses for the data that you will collect.

It can be tempting to create long lists of KPIs and try to evaluate everything you possibly can. In practice, however, this is rarely effective. If you end up measuring everything at once, It is difficult to identify and prioritize problems, and agree a course of action to address them. If conversions from your email campaign are less than you hoped for, is this due to targeting the wrong audience, low open rates, poor body copy, ineffective calls to action - or even a combination of all of these?

In order to address specific issues, It is much more effective to focus on one or two KPIs at a time, with a clear idea of what you are looking to achieve. So, you might choose to focus on your email open rate, and start by testing and improving your subject lines, before moving on to investigate how well your calls to action are motivating click-throughs.

Analytics guru Avinash Kaushik has developed a model for understanding your Digital Marketing and Measurement processes, helping you to prioritize and focus your measurement, testing and enhancement plans. The model takes the Acquisition, Behavior and Conversion frameworks, and asks you to select no more than two goals, with associated targets and KPIs in each section. This forces you to identify your most important goals and KPIs and move forward with those.

In order to decide which of your goals are currently the most important, you can ask yourself questions like:

- "Which of these KPIs would make a significant difference to our bottom line, if we could improve it?"

- This helps you to distinguish between meaningful KPIs, and the metrics that might just be "nice to have," like social media followers.

- Asking "Which KPIs are likely to have the most long-term benefits?" is good for helping you to identify performance improvements that are going to last.

That said, It is also worth seeing if there are any very pressing KPIs or quick fixes that will make an immediate difference. Obviously, if you know about an immediate problem like a wasted paid media spend, fixing this should be a priority. Similarly, if you see quick and easy solutions to problems, you can get those out of the way and move on.

Your aim in defining this model is to create a flexible approach that can be updated at any time. As you improve the performance of a KPI to the point where It is no longer a priority, you can replace it with a new one.

You might choose to create individual measurement models for different departments. For example, customer service teams will have their own priorities and needs, which will be separate from those of sales or marketing, and each of these models can have their own reporting dashboards. However, in order to avoid silos and the risk of teams working on opposing tactics, It is important for everyone to communicate their goals for your digital presence, and recognize opportunities for collaboration.

The world of digital marketing is highly volatile, and your strategies and tactics needs to be flexible in response. It is also quite possible that visitors will exhibit behaviors that you were not expecting, customer journeys could evolve or entirely new audiences could emerge. You will need to design tests for the optimization of your various channels, in order to stay on top of your results and use your measurement model to investigate business- critical KPIs consistently. You should also ensure that your analytics tools are set up from the outset, to be as useful and accurate as possible.

Setting analytics goals relates to measuring the specific conversions or visitor actions that you will be tracking within your analytics tool, such as Google Analytics. These are not the same as your strategic goals, and examples might include macro-conversions like purchases, or micro-conversions like adding items to a shopping cart or sharing your content.

To set them up, look again at your strategic goals and KPIs, and at all of the calls to action within your content. It should be possible to define an analytics goal for each one, and these can be combined with event tracking, to measure behaviors such as the amount of time spent on pages, watching videos, and downloading PDFs. You should by now have a good idea of the relative value of each call to action of your desired outcomes, which will allow you to assign an actual or notional goal value for each case.

You will also want to ensure you have consistent parameters for your campaign tracking. By monitoring the success of every relevant link, you will be able to monitor the impact of various tactics across the channels and calculate your return on investment. Once you start collecting campaign data, you will quickly be able to verify that your tagging mechanisms are consistent and useful.

Defining your multi-channel attribution model is all about recognizing that It is rare for visitors to convert on their first session, and that several channels or paths may influence their transaction. There are a number of methods for assigning credit to each channel, so that you can evaluate its effectiveness, and you will need to decide on the most appropriate method for your business model.

Many companies like to see visitor numbers that exclude employee and developer visits, but internal usage data can provide important information in cases where your website and other channels are extensively used for sales or customer service reports. Since exclusions are done by setting profile filters which cannot be reversed, It is important to set up your data filters carefully, and always retain an unfiltered master copy.

While we are on the topic of filtering, It is also extremely important to segment your analytics reports by specific visitor characteristics, rather than looking at all of your traffic as a single entity. Your work on personas and categories should indicate some visitor segments for setting up your initial analytics reporting, and you will want to add others as you design tests and gain new insights.

In addition to your website analytics, you should be receiving reports from your customer support and call center teams, from your ad campaign tools and agencies, from your partners and affiliates, and from your social media analytics.

Your CRM systems should also show the levels of sales-ready leads that your content is driving, and can help to enhance your understanding of customer journeys and buying cycles. By integrating all of this available data, you should be able to synchronize your findings and gather insights for going forward.

Finally, remember that whilst analytics data tells you what customers do, it does not necessarily explain why they do it, which can leave some large gaps in your ability to fully evaluate your digital marketing success. For more emotion-based feedback, It is helpful to research further, using tools such as customer surveys and focus groups to learn about brand awareness, familiarity and preference, the usability of your website and mobile platforms, and customer satisfaction.

Knowing how to gain actionable intelligence from the results of your activities, and using this to form hypotheses for future testing is a vital part of strategic development. It takes a lot of skill, but it is indispensable. If you do not measure and act on your results, your entire strategy will be nothing more than a series of guesses and estimates, and you will hardly be better off than if you had no strategy at all.

SUMMARY

Even once you have planned your digital strategy and tactics, It is by no means over... Technological and regulatory changes across the channels, from live streaming to voice search, will continue to have an impact on both how campaigns are run, and how customers interact with digital marketing.

In order to stay one step ahead, whatever happens, you will need to keep your strategy flexible and adapt your goals, plans, and activities wherever necessary.

GLOSSARY

Agile: This flexible workflow model, as popularized by the software industry, allows for cross functional and cross-discipline teams to work together to produce the best results in the most efficient way possible, and to prioritize innovating on a continuous basis.

Cost Per Acquisition (CPA) is the total of what it costs your business to acquire a new customer, and It is usually expressed as your marketing costs, divided by the number of customers.

CRM: A process through which a company seeks to manage interactions with customers (both current and potential).

Customer Experience: This refers to how customers perceive your business, as a result of every interaction they have with you - throughout their relationship with the business. Remember that these interactions can take place anywhere: online, offline, directly, and indirectly.

Customer Journey: All of the experiences that a customer has with a company, through the duration of the business relationship.

Daily Stand-Up: A time for members of the team to update each other on their progress and any possible impediments that might be blocking workflow.

Data: Any information that can be collected on things like consumer profiles, consumer behavior, campaign, and ad performance, etc. Data is produced from every interaction that a customer has with your business and can be used as a valuable asset for personalized marketing strategies.

Engagement Strategy: Digital transformation efforts involve a lot of change, and you will need to get employees involved and engaged. Having a detailed engagement strategy will help you to communicate the vision, and is as important as any marketing strategy - you will need to consider who you are talking to, what the message is and how you are getting it across.

Key Performance Indicators (KPIs): A chosen measure of performance for a given business undertaking (e.g., a campaign). KPIs should be set in the early stages of your digital transformation journey to measure success and to promote a culture of learning and adapting.

Lifetime Customer Value: An estimate of the revenue you stand to make from a customer over the entire course of their relationship with you.

Persona is a fictitious profile that brings the characteristics of your target customers to life, to help you plan your interactions with them, and understand their typical needs, behaviors and preferred communication platforms and style.

Return on Ad Spend (ROAS): This is a useful metric for understanding how successful your paid media spending is. It is calculated by dividing your revenue from advertising sources by the cost of that advertising

SEO, or 'Search Engine Optimization', involves optimizing a website using various techniques in order to appear as high up the SERP (Search Engine Results Page) as possible. For a full examination of SEO in theory and practice, check out one of our lessons on the subject.

Situational Analysis: This is an assessment of your business's current status and gives a holistic view of your performance in areas such as customer experience, communication, products and services, and competitor activity.

Waterfall Approach: Project management processes have traditionally followed a 'waterfall approach,' where projects have a pre-defined scope, which is decided at the initial sign-off stage. Work is then passed onto subsequent departments as each stage of development is completed. In many companies, waterfall methods are being replaced by agile workflow processes.

ABOUT JULIAN DELPHIKI

Julian Delphiki chooses to remain pseudonymous, a deliberate decision to safeguard the sanctity of personal identity and ensure that the focus remains firmly on the transformative ideas and practical wisdom he shares. This commitment to privacy paradoxically enhances his message, allowing his insights to resonate without the distractions of personal notoriety. It underscores a philosophical stance that permeates all aspects of his work, from high-level corporate consulting to deeply personal coaching.

For over two decades, Julian has navigated the demanding landscapes of both established corporate giants and agile, cutting-edge startups. This extensive journey has forged him into a multifaceted professional, whose expertise is not merely theoretical but grounded in real-world application. As a seasoned professional, he has honed his skills across various capacities, from intricate project management to executive leadership, consistently delivering results that speak to his unwavering commitment to success. His strategic acumen and remarkable adaptability have made him an invaluable asset, deeply enriching his understanding of organizational dynamics and the challenges faced by modern enterprises. Beyond his corporate endeavors, Julian is the founder and principal consultant of his own firm, where he channels this wealth of experience to help organizations optimize their operations and achieve sustainable growth. His work in this sphere often touches upon areas like optimizing SEO and paid search fundamentals, demonstrating his practical grasp of contemporary business challenges and how they integrate into broader strategic objectives.

Yet, Julian's influence extends far beyond the boardroom. He emerges as a beacon of guidance in the arena of personal development and philosophical exploration. As a dedicated coach, he is passionately committed to fostering self-improvement and a profound understanding of life's intricate philosophies. His coaching philosophy embraces a holistic approach, meticulously intertwining personal growth with deep philosophical introspection. This dual focus allows him to delve into the nuances of critical social science topics such as leadership, resilience, and the relentless pursuit of purpose. With a genuine passion for empowering individuals to unlock their full potential, Julian engages in transformative conversations, providing practical tools that catalyze positive change in individuals' lives. He acts as a true catalyst for transformative journeys, consistently encouraging those around him to embrace the rich complexity of their own narratives.

The seamless blend of Julian Delphiki's professional and personal spheres creates a truly unique mosaic of skills, insights, and a deep commitment to the betterment of individuals and organizations alike. His ability to bridge the strategic demands of the corporate world with the deep introspection required for personal growth provides an extraordinary lens through which to view human behavior, organizational psychology, and societal evolution. This interdisciplinary foundation makes him a compelling voice capable of publishing insightful books on very different topics, united by his overarching mission to facilitate growth and understanding in a complex world. He exemplifies the power of preserving personal privacy while actively contributing to the evolution of both professional and personal landscapes.

OTHER BOOKS BY THE AUTHOR

La abolición del trabajo. BLACK, BOB and DELPHIKI, JULIAN. 2024.

Maestros del hábito. DELPHIKI, JULIAN. 2023.

Modern philosophers. DELPHIKI, JULIAN. 2022

A modern hero. DELPHIKI, JULIAN. 2022.

Folkhorror volume I. DELPHIKI, JULIAN. 2022.

Ad tech and programmatic. DELPHIKI, JULIAN. 2020.

eCommerce 360. English edition. DELPHIKI, JULIAN. 2020.

eCommerce 360. Spanish edition. DELPHIKI, JULIAN. 2020.

Content marketing and online video marketing. DELPHIKI, JULIAN. 2020.

Digital transformation. DELPHIKI, JULIAN. 2020.

Optimizing SEO and paid search fundamentals. DELPHIKI, JULIAN. 2020.

Social media business. DELPHIKI, JULIAN. 2020.

Tales of horror and history. DELPHIKI, JULIAN. 2020.

Web Analytics and Big Data. English edition. DELPHIKI, JULIAN. 2020.

Analítica web y móvil. Spanish edition. DELPHIKI, JULIAN. 2019.

www.ingramcontent.com/pod-product-compliance
Lightning Source LLC
Chambersburg PA
CBHW071423210526
45465CB00001B/507